REFLECT 2

READING & WRITING

KRISTIN SHERMAN

D1568614

Australia · Brazil · Mexico · Singapore · United Kingdom · United States

National Geographic Learning,
a Cengage Company

Reflect 2 Reading & Writing
Author: Kristin Sherman

Publisher: Sherrise Roehr
Executive Editor: Laura Le Dréan
Managing Editor: Jennifer Monaghan
Director of Global Marketing: Ian Martin
Product Marketing Manager: Tracy Baillie
Senior Content Project Manager: Mark Rzeszutek
Media Researcher: Stephanie Eenigenburg
Art Director: Brenda Carmichael
Senior Designer: Lisa Trager
Operations Coordinator: Hayley Chwazik-Gee
Manufacturing Buyer: Mary Beth Hennebury
Composition: MPS Limited

Student Book ISBN: 978-0-357-44849-6
Student Book with Online Practice: 978-0-357-44855-7

National Geographic Learning
200 Pier 4 Boulevard
Boston, MA 02210

Locate your local office at **international.cengage.com/region**

Visit National Geographic Learning online at **ELTNGL.com**
Visit our corporate website at **www.cengage.com**

Printed in China
Print Number: 01   Print Year: 2021

SCOPE AND SEQUENCE

		READING & VOCABULARY EXPANSION
HELPING YOUR COMMUNITY SOCIOLOGY **1** page 2	**Video:** Making sweaters for elephants **Reading 1:** Rescuing animals **Reading 2:** Community heroes	Preview a text Using a dictionary: Example sentences Polysemy: Multiple-meaning words
THE POWER OF FRIENDSHIP PSYCHOLOGY/SOCIOLOGY **2** page 20	**Video:** How to make friends at school **Reading 1:** Casual friends make a difference **Reading 2:** Unlikely friends	Understand paragraph structure Suffix: *-ity* Polysemy: Multiple-meaning words
MUSIC TO THE EARS MUSIC **3** page 38	**Video:** Playing with food **Reading 1:** Learning to the sound of music? **Reading 2:** New in the music world: video game music	Identify supporting sentences and details Onomatopoeia: Words that make noises Using a dictionary: Synonyms
CITIZEN SCIENCE SCIENCE **4** page 56	**Video:** What is citizen science? **Reading 1:** Anyone can be a scientist **Reading 2:** Teen discovers a planet	Guess meaning from context Prefixes: *col-* and *com-* Base words and affixes

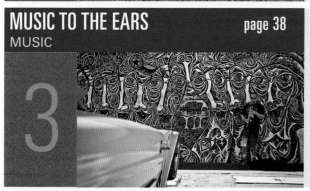

WRITING	GRAMMAR	CRITICAL THINKING	REFLECT ACTIVITIES
Brainstorm	Review of the simple present	Understand reasons	▶ Understand emergencies ▶ Think about your responsibility to your community ▶ Discuss ways to help your community ▶ Evaluate community projects ▶ **UNIT TASK** Write a paragraph about a community project
Organize a paragraph Write topic sentences	Adjectives and comparative adjectives	Support opinions with reasons	▶ Relate ideas to your experience ▶ Think about the importance of friends ▶ Consider different kinds of friends ▶ Connect ideas about friendship ▶ **UNIT TASK** Write a descriptive paragraph about a friend you admire
Write supporting sentences	Count and noncount nouns Quantifiers	Analyze information	▶ Consider how you learn ▶ Write a song or rhyme to remember words ▶ Consider how different kinds of music make you feel ▶ Analyze a type of music ▶ **UNIT TASK** Write an expository paragraph about a song
Write about steps in a process	Simple past	Weigh advantages and disadvantages	▶ Think about how you can get involved ▶ Connect ideas about citizen science ▶ Think about why we explore ▶ Take steps to reach a goal ▶ **UNIT TASK** Write a process paragraph about a citizen science project

FOOD ADVERTISING
MARKETING

page 74

5

Video: Making food look good

Reading 1: What's in a name?

Reading 2: Decisions, decisions

Identify facts and opinions

Word roots: *bene, sect,* and *tract*

Collocations: Adjective + *food*

THE WONDERS OF NATURE
ENVIRONMENTAL SCIENCE

page 92

6

Video: Ha Long Bay

Reading 1: A walk in the woods

Reading 2: World heritage sites

Understand the author's purpose

Prefix: *re-*

Suffixes: *-ing* and *-ive*

LEARNING FROM FAILURE
CAREER STUDIES/PSYCHOLOGY

page 110

7

Video: Facing challenges

Reading 1: From failure to success

Reading 2: Describe your greatest failure

Annotate a text

Formal and informal language

Prefix: *pre-*

SENDING THE RIGHT MESSAGE
BEHAVIORAL SCIENCE/CULTURAL STUDIES

page 128

8

Video: Phone focus

Reading 1: Writing on the Internet

Reading 2: What's the best choice?

Understand pronoun reference

Using a dictionary: Idioms

Collocations: *Send* and *make* + noun

Vocabulary expansion activities   page 146

Appendices   page 154

Index of exam skills and tasks   page 159

Credits   page 160

WRITING	GRAMMAR	CRITICAL THINKING	REFLECT ACTIVITIES
Write concluding sentences	Modals for suggestions and advice	Evaluate writers' claims	▶ Think about your food buying habits ▶ Understand how food labels affect you ▶ Think critically about food choices ▶ Analyze food labels ▶ **UNIT TASK** Write an opinion paragraph about food
Describe data	Infinitives and gerunds	Analyze graphs and charts	▶ Discuss your experiences in nature ▶ Rank the benefits of nature ▶ Identify sites to visit ▶ Investigate World Heritage Sites ▶ **UNIT TASK** Describe a graph or chart about nature
Write coherently	Present perfect	Compare and contrast	▶ Define success and failure ▶ Explore ideas about success and failure ▶ Consider how to be successful in an interview ▶ Compare responses ▶ **UNIT TASK** Write a narrative paragraph about learning from failure
Write an email to a teacher	Review of the present continuous Review of the future	Determine appropriate communication	▶ Analyze communication across generations ▶ Communicate tone in a message ▶ Brainstorm tips for texting ▶ Choose appropriate communication ▶ **UNIT TASK** Write a formal email

CONNECT TO IDEAS

Reflect Reading & Writing features relevant, global content to engage students while helping them acquire the academic language and skills they need. Specially-designed activities give students the opportunity to reflect on and connect ideas and language to their academic, work, and personal lives.

Academic, real-world passages invite students to explore the world while building reading skills and providing ideas for writing.

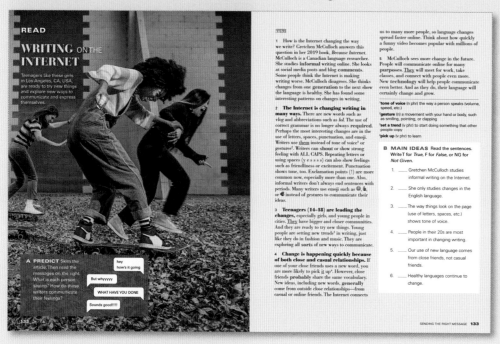

Each unit starts with a **high-interest video** to introduce the theme and generate pre-reading discussion.

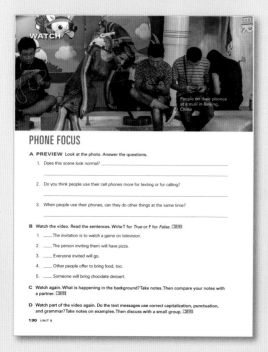

CONNECT TO ACADEMIC SKILLS

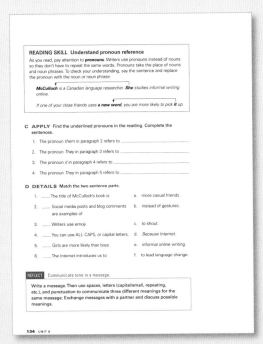

Focused **reading skills** help create confident academic readers.

Reflect activities give students the opportunity to think critically about what they are learning and check their understanding.

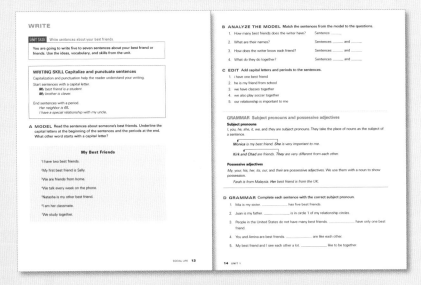

Clear writing models and Analyze the model activities give students a strong framework to improve their writing.

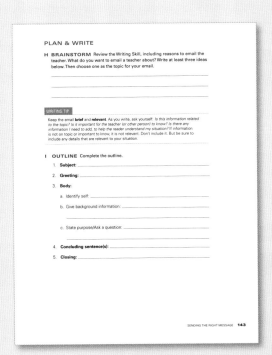

A **step-by-step approach** to the **writing process** along with relevant grammar helps students complete the final writing task with confidence.

CONNECT TO ACHIEVEMENT

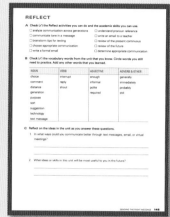

Reflect at the end of the unit is an opportunity for formative assessment. Students review the skills and vocabulary they have gained.

DIGITAL RESOURCES

TEACH lively, engaging lessons that get students to participate actively. The Classroom Presentation Tool helps teachers to present the Student's Book pages, play audio and video, and increase participation by providing a central focus for the class.

LEARN AND TRACK with Online Practice and Student's eBook. For students, the mobile-friendly platform optimizes learning through customized re-teaching and adaptive practice. For instructors, progress-tracking is made easy through the shared gradebook.

ASSESS learner performance and progress with the ExamView® Assessment Suite. For assessment, teachers create and customize tests and quizzes easily using the ExamView® Assessment Suite, available online.

ACKNOWLEDGMENTS

The Authors and Publisher would like to acknowledge the teachers around the world who participated in the development of *Reflect*.

A special thanks to our Advisory Board for their valuable input during the development of this series.

ADVISORY BOARD

Dr. Mansoor S. Almalki, Taif University, Saudi Arabia; **John Duplice**, Sophia University, Japan; **Heba Elhadary**, Gulf University for Science and Technology, Kuwait; **Hind Elyas**, Niagara College, Saudi Arabia; **Cheryl House**, ILSC Education Group, Canada; **Xiao Luo**, BFUS International, China; **Daniel L. Paller,** Kinjo Gakuin University, Japan; **Ray Purdy**, ELS Education Services, USA; **Sarah Symes,** Cambridge Street Upper School, USA.

GLOBAL REVIEWERS

ASIA

Michael Crawford, Dokkyo University, Japan; **Ronnie Hill**, RMIT University Vietnam, Vietnam; **Aaron Nurse**, Golden Path Academics, Vietnam; **Simon Park**, Zushi Kaisei, Japan; **Aunchana Punnarungsee**, Majeo University, Thailand.

LATIN AMERICA AND THE CARIBBEAN

Leandro Aguiar, inFlux, Brazil; **Sonia Albertazzi-Osorio**, Costa Rica Institute of Technology, Costa Rica; **Auricea Bacelar**, Top Seven Idiomas, Brazil; **Natalia Benavides**, Universidad de Los Andes, Colombia; **James Bonilla**, Global Language Training UK, Colombia; **Diego Bruekers Deschamp**, Inglês Express, Brazil; **Josiane da Rosa**, Hello Idiomas, Brazil; **Marcos de Campos Bueno**, It's Cool International, Brazil; **Sophia De Carvalho**, Ingles Express, Brazil; **André Luiz dos Santos**, IFG, Brazil; **Oscar Gomez-Delgado**, Universidad de los Andes, Colombia; **Ruth Elizabeth Hibas**, Inglês Express, Brazil; **Rebecca Ashley Hibas**, Inglês Express, Brazil; **Cecibel Juliao**, UDELAS University, Panama; **Rosa Awilda López Fernández**, School of Languages UNAPEC University, Dominican Republic; **Isabella Magalhães**, Fluent English Pouso Alegre, Brazil; **Gabrielle Marchetti**, Teacher's House, Brazil; **Sabine Mary**, INTEC, Dominican Republic; **Miryam Morron**, Corporación Universitaria Americana, Colombia; **Mary Ruth Popov**, Ingles Express, Ltda., Brazil; **Leticia Rodrigues Resende**, Brazil; **Margaret Simons**, English Center, Brazil.

MIDDLE EAST

Abubaker Alhitty, University of Bahrain, Bahrain; **Jawaria Iqbal**, Saudi Arabia; **Rana Khan**, Algonquin College, Kuwait; **Mick King**, Community College of Qatar, Qatar; **Seema Jaisimha Terry**, German University of Technology, Oman.

USA AND CANADA

Thomas Becskehazy, Arizona State University, AZ; **Robert Bushong**, University of Delaware, DE; **Ashley Fifer**, Nassau Community College, NY; **Sarah Arva Grosik**, University of Pennsylvania, PA; **Carolyn Ho**, Lone Star College-CyFair, TX; **Zachary Johnsrud**, Norquest College, Canada; **Caitlin King**, IUPUI, IN; **Andrea Murau Haraway**, Global Launch / Arizona State University, AZ; **Bobbi Plante**, Manitoba Institute of Trades and Technology, Canada; **Michael Schwartz**, St. Cloud State University, MN; **Pamela Smart-Smith**, Virginia Tech, VA; **Kelly Smith**, English Language Institute, UCSD Extension, CA; **Karen Vallejo**, University of California, CA.

HELPING YOUR COMMUNITY

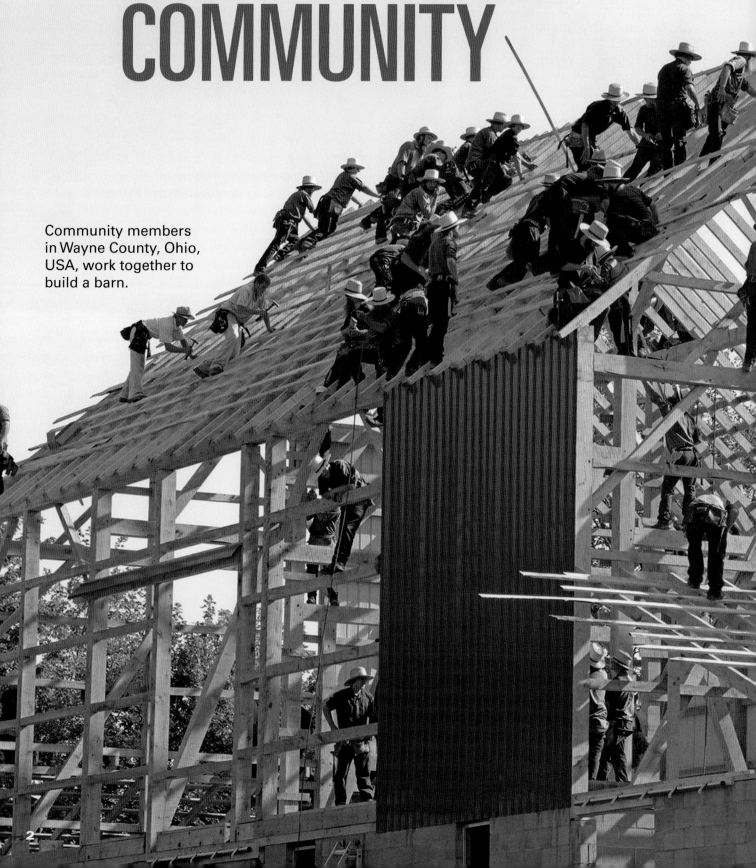

Community members in Wayne County, Ohio, USA, work together to build a barn.

IN THIS UNIT

▶ Understand emergencies

▶ Think about your responsibility to your community

▶ Discuss ways to help your community

▶ Evaluate community projects

▶ Write about a community project

SKILLS

READING
Preview a text

WRITING
Brainstorm

GRAMMAR
Review of the simple present

CRITICAL THINKING
Understand reasons

CONNECT TO THE TOPIC

1. What is happening in the photo?

2. Who is in your community? What does "community" mean to you?

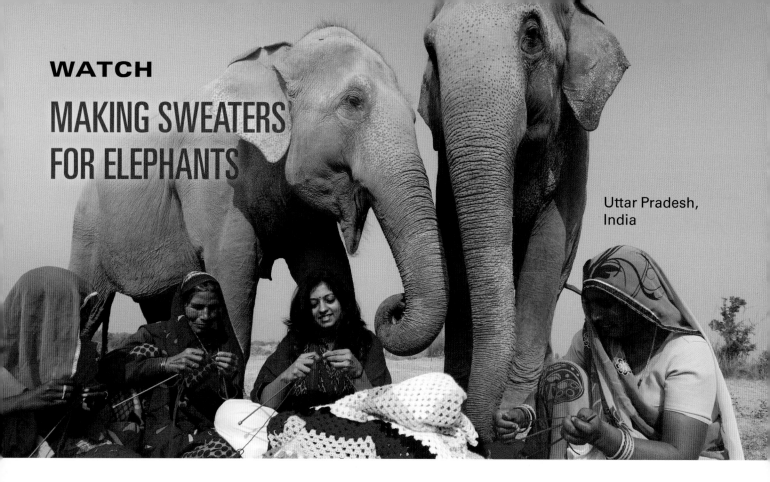

WATCH
MAKING SWEATERS FOR ELEPHANTS

Uttar Pradesh,
India

A PREVIEW Look at the video title and the photo. Answer the questions.

1. What is surprising or interesting about these women and elephants?

2. Why do you think they are making sweaters for elephants?

B Watch the video. Read the sentences. Write T for *True* or F for *False*. ▶ 1.1

1. _____ The people help the elephants when the weather is hot.

2. _____ The women work together to make sweaters for the elephants.

3. _____ The elephants live free outside the city.

C Watch again. Complete the sentences. ▶ 1.1

a. 7	d. Maya	g. legs, back, and neck
b. 21	e. Uttar Pradesh	h. the Elephant Conservation and Care Center
c. 2–3	f. about 9 pounds	

1. The elephants are in _____ in India.

2. A group helps the elephants. The name of the group is _____.

3. Each sweater needs _____ of wool.

4. _____ women make one sweater.

5. It takes _____ weeks to make a sweater.

6. The sweater covers their _____.

7. The name of one elephant is _____. She doesn't want to wear a sweater.

8. The center now has _____ elephants.

PREPARE TO READ

A VOCABULARY Choose the meanings for the words in **bold**.

1. A nice **area** to live is near the park.

   a. part of town or country   b. group of friends   c. busy road

2. Be careful! That street is **dangerous**. There are many car accidents there.

   a. not busy   b. not helpful   c. not safe

3. I wash my car when it is **dirty**.

   a. very hot   b. empty   c. not clean

4. Look! There's a fire truck and a police car. There's an **emergency**!

   a. something new   b. something bad   c. something interesting

5. Soccer players sometimes **hurt** themselves in games because they fall.

   a. score goals   b. exercise hard   c. have pain or injury

6. I don't feel well. I need **medicine**.

   a. doctors and nurses   b. something to stay warm   c. something you take when you are ill

7. People cannot work when they are **sick**.

   a. ill; not feeling well   b. poor   c. sorry about something

8. Our house is small. We need more **space** for our big family.

   a. room, open place   b. fun things to do   c. money

9. Let's stay inside. There's a bad **storm** today, and I don't want to get wet.

   a. rain and wind   b. sunny weather   c. cold, dry weather

10. The weather is **terrible** today. We need to stay inside.

   a. sunny   b. very bad   c. great

REFLECT   Understand emergencies.

You are going to read about what happens in emergencies. Answer the questions. Then discuss with a partner.

1. What are some types of emergencies you know about, such as bad storms?

   _____

2. How do emergencies hurt a community? What helps in an emergency?

   _____

   _____

3. What other things are dangerous to your community?

   _____

This baby hedgehog was rescued or saved from a flood. He is recovering at a rescue center in Kent, England.

READING SKILL Preview a text

Before you read, **preview** the text. When you preview, you look for information that tells you what the text is about. Previewing will help you understand the text better. To preview a text, look at:

▸ photos/visuals   ▸ titles
▸ captions   ▸ subtitles or headings

A PREVIEW Look at the photo and read the caption, title, and headings. What is the article about? Read and check your answer.

RESCUING ANIMALS

1   Every year, there are 400 or more bad **storms** and other natural disasters[1] around the world. These disasters kill 90,000 people. They **hurt** 200 million others. When people know a storm is coming, they leave for shelters[2] or safer **areas**. But what happens to the animals?

Dangers for Animals

2   Storms and other disasters are **dangerous** for animals. Animals cannot usually go to a safe place without help. Storms can hurt animals in different ways. High water in streets and houses can kill dogs and cats. Electrical wires fall in the water and kill fish. Strong winds push birds far away from their homes.

3   Why don't people take their animals with them? Some shelters don't have enough **space** or don't take pets. **Terrible** things can happen. For example, in 2005, 600,000 pets died in New Orleans, Louisiana, USA, during Hurricane Katrina because their owners left them behind. The animals couldn't swim, and they didn't have food.

Ways to Help

4   Many people help animals before, during, and after disasters. Before storms, people take pets and farm animals to animal shelters. During a storm, they look for animals and rescue them. Some people also help wild animals, such as birds, deer, and even koalas in Australia. They give medical care in **emergencies**. After the storm, many pets and wild animals are scared and hurt. High water is very **dirty** and can make animals **sick**. People give the animals **medicine**. They help the animals feel better.

Reasons to Help

5   Because animals are part of our communities, they should get help from people. Of course, most people don't want animals to get hurt. But there are other reasons to help animals in an emergency. First, it's expensive to lose farm animals. Also, dead animals bring disease[3]. In addition, some people die because they stay with their animals during a disaster. For these reasons, taking care of animals during storms is important. This helps the animals, and it helps people, too.

---

[1]**disaster** (n) a terrible act that hurts or kills people, animals, and buildings

[2]**shelter** (n) a building that protects people and animals from bad weather

[3]**disease** (n) an illness

B MAIN IDEAS Read the sentences. Write T for *True*, F for *False*, or NG for *Not Given*. If there is no information in the reading, the answer is NG.

1. _____ Bad storms and other disasters hurt millions of people every year.

2. _____ Animals usually get away before a bad storm comes.

3. _____ Pet owners don't always take their animals with them.

4. _____ People help pets and animals in the zoo.

5. _____ The article gives three reasons to help animals.

CRITICAL THINKING Understand reasons

To understand **reasons**, look for words like *reason* and *because*. Reasons answer the question *Why?*

> **Why** should animals get help during emergencies?
>
> They should get help during emergencies **because** they are part of our community.

C DETAILS Match the reasons to the statements.

Statements

1. ____, ____ People don't bring pets with them.

2. ____, ____ Animals died during Hurricane Katrina.

3. ____, ____ Animals need medicine and help.

4. ____, ____, ____ People should help animals.

Reasons

a. They can't swim.

b. They're scared and hurt.

c. There is no space.

d. There is no food.

e. They are not allowed.

f. It's expensive to lose animals.

g. It stops disease.

h. It helps people.

i. The water is dirty.

REFLECT Think about your responsibility to your community.

Answer the questions. Then discuss your ideas in a small group.

1. In addition to animals, what other parts of your community may need your help in an emergency?

_____

2. What can you do to help them?

_____

3. Why is it important to help all parts of your community?

_____

PREPARE TO READ

A VOCABULARY Read the definitions. Complete the sentences with the correct words.

basic (adj) simple; important	**organization** (n) a group working together
believe (v) to think something is true	**price** (n) the amount of money you pay to buy something
company (n) a business	
earn (v) to get money by working	**project** (n) a piece of work; an assignment
goal (n) a purpose; something to work for	
hero (n) a person who does great things	**sell** (v) to get money for something

1. I have a(n) _____ dictionary. It has only a small number of important words.

2. We want to _____ our car and buy a new one.

3. I work for a(n) _____ that helps elephants. We don't make money, but we do important work.

4. Microsoft is a computer _____. It's a very successful business.

5. She has one _____. She wants to finish school next year.

6. Responsible people _____ that helping others is important.

7. He is a(n) _____ in his community. He helps people find work and a place to live.

8. I don't buy gas there. The _____ is very high. I need to save money.

9. Nick and Taylor work for a big company. They _____ a lot of money.

10. Some classes have a final _____ at the end of the year.

REFLECT Discuss ways to help your community.

You are going to read about people who helped their communities. Think about your community. Discuss the questions with a partner.

1. What does your community need?

2. How can you help your community?

3. How can companies help your community?

Firefighters at work in Meeker, Colorado, USA

COMMUNITY HEROES

A PREVIEW Look at the photo. Read the title, caption, and headings. Check (✓) the things you think the article talks about.

☐ fires   ☐ schools

☐ vacations   ☐ food

☐ homes   ☐ movies

☐ camping   ☐ beaches

READING TIP

When you read, don't worry if you don't understand every word. Read the first time to get the main points.

🎧 1.2

Heroes can be normal people. They see a problem in their community and find a way to help. Here are three stories about community heroes.

Up in Smoke

1   In 2018, a large fire destroyed[1] 14,000 houses in Northern California, USA. About 50,000 people needed new homes. Woody Faircloth wanted to help. He got an RV[2] and filled it with food and clothing. He gave the RV to a family that lost their home. After that, he started an **organization**. It is called RV4CampfireFamily. People give their RVs to the organization or **sell** them at a low **price**. Faircloth fixes the RVs. Then he gives them to families. His **goal** is to find homes for as many families as he can.

Putting Food on the Table

2   Many families move to Malaysia, but they can have a hard time in the new country. They can't always find work. The children sometimes leave school to help their families **earn** money for **basic** things. Three young teachers—Kim Lim, Swee Lin Lee, and Suzanne Ling—wanted to help these children stay in school. So, they started an organization—PichaEats. Families cook food from their home countries. PichaEats sells the food to universities and **companies**. Half of the money goes back to the families. Everybody eats, and the kids stay in school!

Speaking for Girls

3   Zuriel Oduwole **believes** education is very important. She is a young filmmaker[3], still in her teens. When she was nine, Zuriel worked on a **project** for school. She went to Ghana in West Africa to make a film. In Ghana, she saw that many children don't go to school. They need to work. Zuriel's dream[4] is to help children, especially girls in Africa, get an education. She and her younger sisters have an organization called Dream Up, Speak Up, Stand Up. Zuriel talks to girls about staying in school. She also talks to presidents and other world leaders. She tells them it is important for girls to stay in school. Zuriel teaches girls how to make movies so they can tell their own stories. As both a speaker and a teacher, Zuriel is helping girls get an education.

---

[1]**destroy** (v) to pull or break down

[2]**RV** (recreational vehicle) (n) a motor vehicle that people can live in

[3]**filmmaker** (n) someone who makes movies

[4]**dream** (n) something you hope for

B MAIN IDEAS Choose the correct answers.

1. What is the main idea of paragraph 1?

   a. Woody Faircloth gives RVs to people without homes.

   b. Woody Faircloth fights fires in California.

   c. RV4CampfireFamily is an organization that buys and sells RVs.

2. What is the main idea of paragraph 2?

   a. It's hard to move to a new country and find a job.

   b. Cooking food from other countries makes money.

   c. Helping families make money keeps kids in school.

3. What is the main idea of paragraph 3?

   a. Zuriel Oduwole likes to make movies about presidents.

   b. Zuriel and her sisters have an organization called Dream Up, Speak Up, Stand Up.

   c. Zuriel Oduwole helps girls get an education.

C DETAILS Complete the chart with information from each paragraph.

Name of community hero(es)	Name of organization	What they do to help (or How they help)

REFLECT   Evaluate community projects.

Answer the questions. Then discuss with the class. Explain your answers.

1. Which person or people in the article do you think helps their community the most?

2. Which project do you think is the most difficult?

3. Which projects are interesting to you?

WRITE

A book truck in
Oxfordshire, England, U.K.

UNIT TASK Write about a community project.

You are going to write a short paragraph about a community project. It can
be a real program you know about or one you want to start. Use the ideas,
vocabulary, and skills from the unit.

A MODEL Read the paragraph. Underline the name of the project.

The Book Truck

   The Book Truck is a community project in Los Angeles, CA, USA. Some
teenagers don't read very well, and some don't have many books at home. The
Book Truck gives books to teens. It also teaches them to read better. People
help the organization in different ways. Some people give books. Other people
drive the truck to different areas of the city. Others go out with the truck. They
tell kids about different books. The truck is always full of books. The kids choose
any book that they want. With the Book Truck, more kids enjoy reading.

B ANALYZE THE MODEL Complete the sentences from the model.

1. **Project:** The Book Truck is a community project in _____.

2. **Problem:** Some teenagers _____,

   and some _____.

3. **Project actions:** The Book Truck gives _____.

   It also _____.

4. **Three ways people help:**

   a. Some _____.

   b. Other _____.

   c. Others _____.

      They _____.

5. **How the project helps:** With the Book Truck, _____.

GRAMMAR Review of the simple present—*be*

We use the simple present of *be* to describe the subject and to say where it is from, what it is, and its location.

I	***am/'m***	
You/We/They	***are/'re***	*from Ottawa.*
He/She/It	***is/'s***	

I	***am not/'m not***	
You/We/They	***are not/'re not/aren't***	*American.*
He/She/It	***is not/'s not/isn't***	

I	***am/'m***	
You/We/They	***are/'re***	*in Los Angeles.*
He/She/It	***is***	

We often use contractions when we speak, but less often when we write.

C GRAMMAR Complete the sentences with the simple present of *be*.

1. The river _____ strong and fast.

2. The animals _____ scared but safe.

3. I _____ (not) at a shelter.

4. The organization _____ (not) in Ottawa.

5. We _____ happy to help.

6. Their goals _____ on the website.

7. You _____ (not) a terrible cook.

8. She _____ a young filmmaker.

9. Many young girls _____ (not) in school.

10. It _____ important for children to get an education.

GRAMMAR Review of the simple present

We use the simple present of other verbs to talk about regular activities or repeated actions in the present, and for general truths or facts.

With *he*, *she*, and *it*, regular verbs have an *-s* ending.
Some verbs are irregular: *have/has*, *go/goes*, *do/does*.

I/You/We/They	**make**	*food for people.*
He/She/It	**makes**	

I/You/We/They	**do not/don't make**	*food for people.*
He/She/It	**does not/doesn't make**	

We often use the simple present with adverbs of frequency, such as *usually* or *sometimes*.

Mia **sometimes goes** to the park on weekends.

D GRAMMAR Underline the simple present verbs in the model in activity A.

Ottawa River,
Ottawa, Canada

Old fishing nets hurt coral reefs.

E GRAMMAR Complete the paragraph with the simple present of the verbs.

end up	help	hurt	make	pay	take	use	want

Helping Beach Communities with Net-Works™

Net-Works™ is a community project in the Philippines. Fishermen

¹_____ plastic nets to catch fish. There are now many old fishing

nets in the ocean. These nets ²_____ the fish and the coral reefs.

They also ³_____ on the beaches. People ⁴_____

(not) to go to the beaches. Net-Works™ ⁵_____ people money to

collect the nets. They ⁶_____ the nets out of the ocean and off the

beaches. Then they ⁷_____ carpets from the nets. This program

⁸_____ the ocean and the people in the community.

F GRAMMAR Answer the questions. Use the simple present.

1. Do people in your community help each other? What do they do?

   _____

2. Does your community have a hero? What does he/she do?

   _____

G EDIT Read the paragraph. Find and correct five errors with the simple present.

TechWorks

Do you believe we should help others? I think it's very important. I works

for an organization called TechWorks. TechWorks help young people learn about

science. Some students not are good with computers. TechWorks haves basic

classes about computers. Students use computers for their projects. The

normal hours is after school, from 3 p.m. to 9 p.m., but sometimes it is open

later. Our goal at TechWorks is science education for everyone.

PLAN & WRITE

WRITING SKILL Brainstorm

Before you write, **brainstorm** ideas. When you brainstorm, you do the following:

1. Think of as many ideas as you can.
2. Write the ideas down.
3. Don't think about whether an idea is good or bad—just write it for now.
4. Begin to make the list smaller, choosing the best idea(s).

H APPLY Follow the instructions.

1. Think about the video and articles in the unit for ideas. What problems do the people help with? _____

    _____

2. Now list the problems in your community. _____

    _____

3. Which community problem is the most important? Choose one to write about.

    _____

4. Make a list of different ways to help with the problem. Then decide which is the most helpful.

    _____

    _____

    _____

I PLAN Use the chart to organize your ideas. You can write about a project you know or one you want to start.

What is the name of the project?	
What problem does it help?	
List three things it does/people do on this project.	1. _____ 2. _____ 3. _____
How does the project help the community?	

J FIRST DRAFT Use the model in activity A and the information from activity I to write a first draft of your paragraph.

K REVISE Use this list as you write your second draft.

☐ Do you name the project in the first sentence?

☐ Do you name the problem?

☐ Do you list three things the project does?

☐ Do you use the simple present correctly?

☐ Do you say how the project helps the community?

> **WRITING TIP**
>
> Use a **capital letter** at the beginning of each sentence. Use **ending punctuation**, such as periods and question marks, at the end of each sentence.

L EDIT Use this list as you write your final draft.

☐ Do you use -s endings with *he*, *she*, and *it*?

☐ Do you use correct capitalization?

☐ Do you use correct punctuation?

M FINAL DRAFT Reread your final draft and correct any errors. Then submit it to your teacher.

REFLECT

A Check (✓) the Reflect activities you can do and the academic skills you can use.

☐ understand emergencies

☐ think about your responsibility to your community

☐ discuss ways to help your community

☐ evaluate community projects

☐ write about a community project

☐ preview a text

☐ brainstorm

☐ review of the simple present

☐ understand reasons

B Check (✓) the vocabulary words from the unit that you know. Circle words you still need to practice. Add any other words that you learned.

NOUN	VERB	ADJECTIVE	ADVERB & OTHER
area	believe	basic	
company	earn	dangerous	
emergency	hurt	dirty	
goal	sell	sick	
hero		terrible	
medicine			
organization			
price			
project			
space			
storm			

C Reflect on the ideas in the unit as you answer these questions.

1. What is the most helpful thing you learned about community in this unit?

_____

_____

3. What ideas or skills in this unit will be most useful to you in the future?

_____

_____

THE POWER OF FRIENDSHIP

A group of orangutans laugh together.

IN THIS UNIT

▶ Relate ideas to your experience

▶ Think about the importance of friends

▶ Consider different kinds of friends

▶ Connect ideas about friendship

▶ Write a paragraph about a friend you admire

SKILLS

READING
Understand paragraph structure

WRITING
Organize a paragraph

Write topic sentences

GRAMMAR
Adjectives and comparative adjectives

CRITICAL THINKING
Support opinions with reasons

CONNECT TO THE TOPIC

1. What is unusual about the photo? How does it make you feel?

2. Why are friends important?

HOW TO MAKE FRIENDS AT SCHOOL

A ACTIVATE What kinds of activities and clubs are there at college? Work with a partner to make a list.

English Club, soccer team

B Match the words with their definitions.

1. _____ brave
2. _____ dorm (dormitory)
3. _____ nervous
4. _____ similar
5. _____ stressful

a. almost the same
b. causing worry or anxiety
c. a building where students live
d. not afraid of danger; without fear
e. worried about a future event

C Watch the video. Put the ideas in the order you hear them. ▶ 2.1

a. _____ Be yourself.
b. _____ Be open.
c. _____ Be brave.

d. _____ Meet classmates.
e. _____ Join in.

D What can you do to make more friends at your school? Discuss with a partner.

First year students buy art for their dorm rooms at Aberystwyth University, Wales, UK.

PREPARE TO READ

A VOCABULARY Read the definitions. Complete the sentences with the correct words.

activity (n) a planned event; something to do	**introduce** (v) to present a person, thing, or idea for the first time
become (v) to grow into; to be	**positive** (adj) hopeful; helpful
casual (adj) informal; not serious	**research** (n) a study of information
connect (v) to join	**stranger** (n) a person you don't know
improve (v) to make better	**variety** (n) many different kinds of something

1. Social media and email _____ me to my friends in other cities.

2. Students often do _____ in the library or online. It helps them learn more about a topic.

3. We want to _____ our English. We practice new vocabulary words.

4. Let me _____ you to my friend Hakim. He is a new student.

5. Tyler is a very _____ person. He likes people and is usually happy.

6. When you start a new class or job, everybody is a(n) _____.

7. Kayla wants to _____ a doctor.

8. I enjoy playing tennis. It's a great _____ to do with others.

9. My relationship with my teacher is _____. I call her by her first name.

10. The library has a(n) _____ of books about sports.

REFLECT Relate ideas to your experience.

Before you read about different kinds of friendship, think about your own experience. Answer the questions. Then discuss with a partner.

1. What activities do you enjoy with friends and family?

   _____

2. What is the difference between close friends and casual friends?

   _____

3. Do you like to introduce yourself to strangers? Explain.

   _____

READ

A PREVIEW Answer the questions.

1. Read the title and the first sentence of each paragraph. What do you think the article is about?

   a. Ways best friends help us

   b. Ways to make casual friends

   c. Ways casual friends help us

2. Look at the photo and read the caption. What does it show? How does it connect to the article?

READING SKILL
Understand paragraph structure

A paragraph is a group of sentences on one topic. The **topic** of a paragraph is what the paragraph is about, for example, *friends* or *meeting new people.*

The **main idea** of a paragraph is the most important idea the writer wants to communicate.

The sentence that tells the main idea is the **topic sentence**. It is usually the first or second sentence in the paragraph.

The other sentences in a paragraph **support**, or give more information about, the main idea.

The last, or **concluding sentence**, often says the main idea again.

Understanding the structure of a paragraph helps you understand a reading.

Customers talk with the farmers at a farm stand in Maui, Hawaii, USA. This man is getting his pizza to go.

CASUAL FRIENDS MAKE A DIFFERENCE 🔊 2.1

1   Everyone knows that friendships are important. We all need our best friends. Best friends share good times and bad. We tell our close friends our secrets[1]. But what about **casual** friends? They are the friends we see only now and then. They are our classmates, the customers at the cafe, or the neighbor walking his dog. When we have a lot of casual friends, it **improves** our lives in several ways.

2   First, casual friends make us happy. We talk to them at the bus stop or the farm stand. We feel like we are part of a community[2]. **Research** shows that the more casual friends we have, the more **positive** we feel. In one study, students felt much happier when they talked to more classmates than usual. These low-key[3] friendships **become** very important as we get older. We have the most friends at age 25, but the number goes down after that. As we get older, we have fewer friendships and can feel alone. But we feel less lonely when we have many casual friends.

3   Second, casual friends **connect** us to other groups of people. They tell us about fun **activities** and possible jobs. In fact, people are 58 percent more likely to get a job through a casual friend than a close friend. Casual friends **introduce** us to their other friends. They help when we want to know about good restaurants or exciting movies. Research shows that casual friendships are a good way to spread[4] all kinds of information.

4   Finally, casual friends introduce us to a **variety** of new ideas. Our best friends often think like us, but casual friends may have very different opinions. When we talk to different people, we learn new ways of seeing the world. It makes us kinder and more understanding.

5   To have a better life, make more casual friends. Talk more to **strangers**. These people can become casual friends. Over time, casual friends can become close friends. And the more friends you have, the happier you'll be. Casual friends may be the secret to a happy life.

---

[1]**secret** (n) information other people do not know

[2]**community** (n) a group of people with the same interests or way of life

[3]**low-key** (adj) informal; not serious; casual

[4]**spread** (v) to reach a large area or group

B APPLY Underline the main idea in paragraphs 2–4 of the article. Then underline any concluding sentences that say the main idea again.

C MAIN IDEAS The article has five paragraphs. Match the paragraph number to the correct heading.

a. _____ New ideas

b. _____ Who are casual friends?

c. _____ Connecting with others

d. _____ A better life

e. _____ Friends and happiness

D DETAILS Read the sentences. Write T for *True,* F for *False,* or NG for *Not Given.*

1. _____ We tell our casual friends our secrets.

2. _____ Someone at the bus stop can be a casual friend.

3. _____ Casual friends make our lives better.

4. _____ People have the most friends at age 40.

5. _____ Most people have about 15 casual friends.

6. _____ Casual friends introduce us to people and activities.

7. _____ Our casual friends usually think the same way we do.

CRITICAL THINKING Support opinions with reasons

Opinions are stronger when you give **reasons**. For example, if you think family relationships are more important than friendships, give reasons for that opinion. One reason might be that your family knows you better than anyone else.

REFLECT Think about the importance of friends.

Answer the questions. Then discuss your ideas in a small group.

1. Do you think best friends or casual friends are more important? Give reasons.

_____

_____

2. In what ways do your friends change you, your ideas, and your life in general?

_____

_____

PREPARE TO READ

A VOCABULARY Complete the sentences with the correct form of the words.

| afterward (adv) | contact (n) | find out (v phr) | happen (v) | strange (adj) |
| common (adj) | decide (v) | fit (adj) | opinion (n) | successful (adj) |

1. I don't have too much information about it, but I can _____.

2. My best friend loves pizza with bananas. I think that's _____.

3. Jenna and I have some _____ interests. We both like to read and play tennis.

4. Something exciting always _____ in a good soccer game.

5. My sister exercises five days a week. She's very _____.

6. Many high school students _____ to go to college, but some choose to get a job.

7. They work until 5:00 p.m. _____, they go home and eat dinner.

8. What's your _____ of this class? Do you think it's interesting?

9. Jacob doesn't do well on projects. His projects are not usually _____.

10. I don't have a lot of _____ with my childhood friends. We rarely talk.

B PERSONALIZE Complete the sentences. Then compare answers with a partner.

1. On most days, I have a lot of **contact** with _____.

2. To be more **fit**, I _____.

3. I want to **find out** more about _____.

4. _____ helps me **decide** my weekend plans.

5. I feel **successful** when I _____.

REFLECT Consider different kinds of friends.

You are going to read about two friends who are very different from each other. Answer the questions. Then discuss with your class.

1. Is it important to have friends with the same opinions, or friends who have different ideas?

   _____

2. What can you do when you and a friend don't share the same opinion on something?

   _____

UNLIKELY FRIENDS  2.2

1   An 83-year-old store owner and a 14-year-old high-school student in Singapore may sound like a **strange** pair, but they are good friends. Bill Teoh and Kieyron Maldini are part of the Back To School project. Back To School matches an older person with a teenager for 10 weeks to see what **happens**. **Afterward**, the project makes a movie about the pair.

2   Mr. Teoh and Kieyron are different in many ways. Mr. Teoh lives with his son and grandchildren, but he doesn't have much contact with them. He is **successful** in many other ways. He has a small store, is an actor[1] on a TV show, and exercises every day. Mr. Teoh is very good at bowling and badminton. He doesn't have a good **opinion** of most teenagers. He seems unfriendly. Kieyron, on the other hand, seems very friendly. He plays a lot of video games. Kieyron doesn't exercise very much. He is not very **fit** at all.

3   The two **find out** they have **common** interests. One is comic books. Mr. Teoh sells comic books in his store, including Spider-Man. Kieyron is a fan of Spider-Man. Mr. Teoh and Kieyron talk about superheroes. One day, Kieyron asks Mr. Teoh to come to his house for lunch. They eat chicken curry and play video games, two things they both enjoy.

A team of superheroes from a comic book

A PREVIEW Answer the questions.

1. *Unlikely* means "strange or unusual." Read the first sentence of the article. Why are these friends unlikely?

2. What common interest do you think they have?

4   Their relationship changes the two new friends. Mr. Teoh **decides** to help Kieyron. He takes him to his TV show. Mr. Teoh introduces Kieyron to the other actors. Mr. Teoh also helps the teen with physical[2] activities. This helps Kieyron on the school fitness test. At the end of the 10 weeks, both Kieyron and Mr. Teoh have better fitness, and they are both happier. They are unlikely, but good, friends.

---

[1]**actor** (n) a person who performs in plays, television shows, or movies

[2]**physical** (adj) related to the body

B MAIN IDEAS Underline the main idea of each paragraph.

C MAIN IDEAS The article has four paragraphs. Match the paragraph number to the correct heading.

a. _____ Differences between Mr. Teoh and Kieyron

b. _____ The Back To School project

c. _____ Good things their friendship caused

d. _____ Things Mr. Teoh and Kieyron have in common

D DETAILS Read the list of activities. Who likes to do them? Write MT for *Mr. Teoh*, K for *Kieyron*, or B for *Both*. Share your ideas with a partner.

1. _____ act

2. _____ exercise

3. _____ read comic books

4. _____ play badminton

5. _____ go bowling

6. _____ play video games

E DETAILS Complete the information with one word or phrase. You may use words more than once.

actor	eighties	fit	grandchildren	store owner	video games
badminton	exercise	friendly	happier	teens	

		Bill Teoh	**Kieyron Maldini**
1.	Age	is in his _____	is in his _____
2.	Living situation	lives with his son and _____	lives with his family
3.	Adjectives	seems unfriendly	seems _____
4.	Job(s)	is a(n) _____ is a(n) _____ on a TV show	is a student
5.	Fitness/Exercise	exercises every day is very _____	doesn't like to _____ isn't _____
6.	Interests	likes bowling, _____, _____, comics, and superheroes	likes _____, comics, and superheroes
7.	Changes because of project	is more _____ is _____	is more _____ is _____

REFLECT   Connect ideas about friendship.

Discuss the questions with a partner. Use ideas from the two articles and your own experience.

1. What are some ways to make friends with people who are different from you?

2. After reading the articles, are you more likely to try to meet people who are different from you?

3. American playwright Tennessee Williams wrote: "Life is partly what we make it, and partly what it is made by the friends we choose." Do you agree?

WRITE

UNIT TASK Write a paragraph about a friend you admire.

You are going to write a paragraph to describe a friend you admire (or have a good opinion of). You will write about your friend's appearance, personality, and actions. Use the ideas, vocabulary, and skills from the unit.

A MODEL Read the paragraph. Underline the topic sentence.

My Friend Hananah

I admire my friend Hananah very much. She is tall and strong. She has a nice smile. More importantly, she is smart, kind, and funny. She is a better student than I am and helps me study. When I am sad or lonely, she is there for me. With Hananah, I feel more positive. I enjoy spending time with her because she makes me laugh. My life is happier because Hananah is my friend.

WRITING SKILL   Organize a paragraph

You learned that a **paragraph** is a group of sentences. A paragraph has three parts:
- ▶ The **topic sentence** tells the reader the writer's main idea. It is a one-sentence summary of the paragraph.
- ▶ The **supporting sentences** explain and give more information about the main idea presented in the topic sentence.
- ▶ The **concluding sentence** is the last sentence. It often states the main idea again in different words.

Plan these three parts before you write. This will help you organize your paragraph.

B ANALYZE THE MODEL Complete the outline of the model paragraph.

1. **Topic sentence:** I admire _____.

2. **Supporting sentences:**

   a. Physical appearance (what friend looks like): _____

   b. Personality (type of person friend is): _____

   c. Actions (what friend does): _____

   _____

3. **Concluding sentence:** My life is _____.

C APPLY Read the sentences from a paragraph. Write T for *Topic sentence,* S for *Supporting sentence,* or C for *Concluding sentence.* Then write the sentences as a paragraph.

A Great Soccer Player

1. _____ He helps his teammates on and off the field.

2. _____ Hiro is very strong and fast.

3. _____ I admire my friend Hiro because he is a great soccer player.

4. _____ He practices every day.

5. _____ For these reasons, I think Hiro is an excellent soccer player.

6. _____ Hiro also goes to the gym.

WRITING SKILL   Write topic sentences

A **topic sentence** has two parts:
  ▸ the topic (what the paragraph is about)
  ▸ the controlling idea

The **controlling idea** guides the topic in one direction.

        topic   controlling idea
First, casual friends make us happy.

From this sentence, we know that the paragraph is about casual friends. Specifically, it is about how they make us happy.

    controlling idea   topic
I admire my friend Hananah very much.

The paragraph is about Hananah. Specifically, it is about how the writer admires her.

D APPLY Read the topic sentences. Circle the topic. Underline the controlling idea.

1. My friend Maya is a very good student.

2. A good friend helps you in many ways.

3. Friendship teaches us many things.

4. A good friend is not hard to find.

E APPLY Choose a topic sentence from activity D for the paragraph. Compare ideas with a partner.

A Good Friend

_____ First, she listens to your problems. She also makes you feel better when you are sad. A good friend introduces you to other people. Also, she laughs at your bad jokes. A good friend makes your life better.

GRAMMAR Adjectives

We use **adjectives** to describe nouns (people, places, things). Adjectives come before nouns.

adj. + noun   adj. + noun

She has **good** ideas. A **good** friend listens well.

Adjectives can also follow *be*.

be + adj.

I am **sad.**

Adjectives are never plural.

They are **olds** friends.

F GRAMMAR Underline the noun and circle the adjective in the first sentence. Then complete the second sentence with *adjective + noun.*

1. The woman is friendly. She is a ___friendly woman_____.

2. This story is interesting. It is an _____.

3. My parents are great. I have _____.

4. Some friends are caring. Miko and Hari are _____.

5. Some clothes are colorful. My friend Ana wears _____.

6. Some people are lonely. _____ need more casual friends.

GRAMMAR Comparative adjectives

We use **comparative adjectives** to show the difference between two people or things.

For one-syllable adjectives, we add **-er**. If the adjective ends in *y*, change it to *i* and add *-er.*
Wade is **smarter than** Jessica.
Wade is funny, but Jessica is **funnier**.

Note: We use *than* if the second item is included in the comparison.

For most adjectives with two or more syllables, we use **more** + adjective.
caring → more caring   important → more important

Some adjectives have irregular comparative forms.
good → better   bad → worse

G GRAMMAR Complete the sentences with the comparative form of the adjectives. Use *than* if needed.

1. Mr. Teoh is _____ (old) Kieyron.

2. Kieyron and Mr. Teoh are _____ (happy) now.

3. My sister's hair is _____ (red) my hair.

4. Adam is _____ (successful) his brother Jason.

5. Some of my friends are _____ (good) students than others.

6. Madison is _____ (nice) Olivia, but they are both funny.

H GRAMMAR Complete the sentences with your ideas. Use adjectives, including comparative adjectives.

1. A good friend is always _____.

2. My best friend has _____.

3. I admire people who are _____ than other people.

4. Friends can have problems if one friend is _____ than the other.

I EDIT Find and correct four errors with adjectives and comparative adjectives.

My Friend Artun

I admire my friend Artun very much. He is a teacher excellent and always helps his students. He has excitings ideas about teaching. His classes are interestinger than most. A teacher has a difficult job, but it seems easy for Artun. He is more good at it than other teachers. Artun is a great teacher and a wonderful person.

PLAN & WRITE

J BRAINSTORM Write the names of three friends you admire in the chart.
Take notes to describe each. Use the adjectives below for ideas.

Name: _____	Name: _____	Name: _____

Physical appearance	Personality	
athletic	brave	intelligent
attractive	clever	interesting
fit	friendly	kind
healthy	funny	patient
powerful	helpful	positive
strong	hard-working	successful

WRITING TIP

Use a dictionary or thesaurus to find **synonyms**, or words that have the same or almost the same meaning. For example, *caring* is like *helpful* or *kind*. Synonyms make your writing more interesting.

Who can you write the most about? Choose one friend. _____

K OUTLINE Complete the outline.

1. **Topic sentence:** I admire my friend _____

2. **Supporting sentences:**

   a. Physical appearance: _____

   b. Personality: _____

   c. Action 1: _____

   _____

   d. Action 2: _____

   _____

3. **Concluding sentence:** _____

   _____

L FIRST DRAFT Use the model in activity A and your outline to write a first draft of your paragraph.

M REVISE Use this list as you write your second draft.

☐ Does your topic sentence introduce the main idea of your paragraph?

☐ Do you describe your friend's physical appearance?

☐ Do you describe your friend's personality?

☐ Do you give examples of your friend's actions?

☐ Does the paragraph have a concluding sentence?

N EDIT Use this list as you write your final draft.

☐ Do you use adjectives and comparative adjectives correctly?

☐ Do your subjects and verbs agree?

☐ Do you spell all the words correctly?

☐ Do you use correct capitalization and punctuation?

O FINAL DRAFT Reread your final draft and correct any errors. Then submit it to your teacher.

REFLECT

A Check (✓) the Reflect activities you can do and the academic skills you can use.

☐ relate ideas to your experience   ☐ understand paragraph structure

☐ think about the importance of friends   ☐ organize a paragraph

☐ consider different kinds of friends   ☐ write topic sentences

☐ connect ideas about friendship   ☐ adjectives and comparative adjectives

☐ write a paragraph about a friend you admire   ☐ support opinions with reasons

B Check (✓) the vocabulary words from the unit that you know. Circle words you still need to practice. Add any other words that you learned.

NOUN	VERB	ADJECTIVE	ADVERB & OTHER
activity	become	casual	afterward
contact	connect	common	
opinion	decide	fit	
research	find out	positive	
stranger	happen	strange	
variety	improve	successful	
	introduce		

C Reflect on the ideas in the unit as you answer these questions.

1. What will you do to develop more casual relationships?

_____

_____

2. What ideas or skills in this unit will be most useful to you in the future?

_____

_____

UNIT 3 | MUSIC TO THE EARS

A street musician plays the saxophone along the East Side Gallery wall in Berlin, Germany. About 100 artists from all over the world painted this section of the wall.

IN THIS UNIT

▶ Consider how you learn

▶ Write a song or rhyme to remember words

▶ Consider how different kinds of music make you feel

▶ Analyze a type of music

▶ Write a paragraph about a song

SKILLS

READING
Identify supporting sentences and details

WRITING
Write supporting sentences

GRAMMAR
Count and noncount nouns

Quantifiers

CRITICAL THINKING
Analyze information

CONNECT TO THE TOPIC

1. How is the man in the photo using music?

2. In what ways do you use music?

WATCH

PLAYING WITH FOOD

A PREVIEW Look at the photo. Answer the questions.

1. What kinds of instruments do you think these are? _____

2. Why do you think people make and play these "instruments"? _____

B Watch the video. Then read the sentences. Write T for *True* or F for *False.* ▶ 3.1

1. _____ The musicians want the music to be funny.

2. _____ The first instrument was the tomato.

3. _____ The orchestra is very new.

4. _____ There are six types of instruments.

5. _____ A pepper is ready to play.

6. _____ It takes two to three hours to make the instruments.

C Watch again. Answer the questions. ▶ 3.1

1. What instruments are easy to make? _____

2. What do they do to make some of the instruments? _____

3. What do they do with the vegetables they don't use as instruments?

    _____

PREPARE TO READ

A VOCABULARY Read the sentences. Write the words in **bold** next to their definitions.

    a. People think I play the piano, but **actually** I play the guitar.

    b. Many restaurants play music in the **background**.

    c. I don't like all music. I only like **certain** kinds of music, such as pop.

    d. This article is very difficult. I need to **concentrate** to understand it.

    e. My grandfather's **memory** isn't very good anymore, but he can remember some things.

    f. It's very **noisy** outside. I hear cars, music, and people talking.

    g. You have to be **quiet** in the library. It's hard to study when people talk.

    h. Listen to the sentences on the audio. Then **repeat** the sentences you hear.

    i. People usually think hard when they **solve** problems.

    j. What's that **sound**? Is it music?

1. _____ (n) something you can hear

2. _____ (n) something you can see or hear behind something else

3. _____ (adv) really; in truth

4. _____ (n) the ability to remember

5. _____ (v) to say again

6. _____ (adj) with little noise or sound

7. _____ (v) to find an answer to something

8. _____ (v) to focus attention; to think hard about something

9. _____ (adj) some; a limited amount

10. _____ (adj) full of sound; not quiet

REFLECT Consider how you learn.

You are going to read about music and learning. Consider your own learning. Then compare ideas with a partner.

1. Read the sentences. Rate yourself from 1 to 3 (1 = disagree, 2 = not sure, 3 = agree).

    _____ I solve problems well.   _____ I need a quiet place to concentrate.

    _____ I have a good memory.   _____ I work better with background sounds.

    _____ I usually have a study plan.   _____ I am a creative thinker.

2. Do you want to improve how you study? If so, how?

    _____

READ

LEARNING TO THE SOUND OF MUSIC?

British artist Stephen Wiltshire listens to music as he works on a picture of New York, NY, USA. He draws entirely from memory.

A PREDICT Read the title and look at the photo and caption.

1. How do you think the photo connects to the blog post?

2. Check (✓) the ideas you think the blog post talks about. Then read and check your answers.

☐ learning vocabulary   ☐ helping classmates
☐ solving problems   ☐ background music
☐ writing paragraphs   ☐ songs and rhymes
☐ learning the alphabet   ☐ using no music at all

1   What's the best way to study for a big test? And what's the best way to remember information? I have an important test next week and want to try something new, maybe music. The research on music and **memory** is interesting. Music can help you learn and remember in **certain** ways.

Listening to background music

2   Music in the **background** may help learning, but it depends on the person and the music. One Canadian study shows that students with good memories learn vocabulary words better when they listen to **quiet** music. Students with poor memories do worse. The kind of music is also important. It should be soft and gentle. Even people with good memories learn and remember less if they listen to **noisy**, angry music.

3   Another study in the U.K. and Sweden looks at music and **solving** problems. In the study, they ask people to solve a problem and think creatively. If there is any background music at all, people do worse on the task. But when people work with background conversation, it does not hurt their problem solving. If you have to **concentrate**, background noise may be OK, but music hurts rather than helps.

Using rhymes and songs

4   Certain kinds of music **actually** help us remember information. Songs and rhymes are very good at this. In a study at the University of Edinburgh, students learned words in Hungarian much more quickly when they put them in a song. It's not the music itself; it's the structure[1]. Songs **repeat** both **sounds** and beats[2]. The end of each line in a song often has the same sound, or rhyme. The rhyme helps your memory. Do you know the alphabet song that begins: *A B C D E F G, H I J K, L M N O P?* The beats and the rhyming of *G* and *P* help children to remember the letters.

5   What is the best plan to study for my test? I think a quiet place will help me learn difficult information, and I'll make a song to help me learn my new vocabulary words. What study plan do you think is best for you?

---

[1]**structure** (n) the way parts are put together
[2]**beat** (n) the regular, stressed sound in music

B MAIN IDEAS Match the two sentence parts to complete the main ideas.

1. Quiet background music might help

    _____

2. Don't listen to background music

    _____

3. You can remember information like the alphabet _____

    a. with rhymes and songs.
    b. you learn vocabulary.
    c. when you want to solve problems.

C MAIN IDEAS The blog post has five paragraphs. Match the paragraph number to the correct topic.

a. _____ How different kinds of music help or hurt vocabulary learning

b. _____ How the writer plans to study

c. _____ The reason the writer is talking about music

d. _____ Solving problems and listening to music

e. _____ Why songs help us remember information

READING SKILL   Identify supporting sentences and details

The topic sentence of a paragraph gives the main idea. Other sentences help, or support, the main idea. They give more information. These **supporting sentences** are often reasons, examples, or other details.

Main idea: *Music can change the way you feel.*
Supporting sentences:

> *Quiet music can relax you because your heart follows the beat of the music.* (reason)
>
> *For example, parents often sing quiet songs to babies to help them sleep.* (example)
>
> *Quiet music makes some people sad, but it gives most people a positive feeling.* (other detail)

D DETAILS The blog post has five paragraphs. Match the paragraph number with each detail. You can write a paragraph number more than once.

a. _____ Background conversation and solving problems

b. _____ The alphabet song as an example

c. _____ The writer's plan for vocabulary

d. _____ The University of Edinburgh study of learning Hungarian

e. _____ The reason the writer is writing the blog post

f. _____ A study in the U.K. and Sweden on music and thinking

g. _____ Students with good memories

h. _____ Gentle vs. angry music

LEARNING TIP

Try to identify how you learn best. When you know how you learn and remember information, you can prepare for tests better.

E Answer the questions. Then discuss with a partner.

1. Do you listen to music when you study? Explain.

_____

2. What rhymes or songs do you know about that help with memory?

_____

REFLECT   Write a song or rhyme to remember words.

> Work in a small group. Write a new song or rhyme, or use one you know, such as "Happy Birthday", to help you remember four or five of the vocabulary words. Take turns practicing your songs or rhymes.

PREPARE TO READ

A VOCABULARY Complete the sentences with the correct words.

click (n)	culture (n)	however (adv)	popular (adj)	useful (adj)
communicate (v)	experience (n)	modern (adj)	type (n)	volume (n)

1. Do you like older kinds of music or more _____ music?

2. Music, food, and art are part of a country's _____.

3. When I close the door, I listen for a soft _____.

4. That music is very loud. Please turn the _____ down.

5. Many people like K-pop. It's a(n) _____ kind of music from South Korea.

6. My trip to New Zealand was a great _____. I remember it very well.

7. Jazz is one _____ of music, but there are many other kinds.

8. I don't listen to music when I study. _____, I listen to music when I exercise.

9. Speaking English is _____. You can do many things if you know the language.

10. Most colleges _____ with students by email. Some also send text messages.

B PERSONALIZE Answer the questions. Then compare answers with a partner.

1. What **types** of music are **popular** in your **culture**? Are they **modern**?

2. Tell about one **experience** you remember when you hear a certain song.

3. How do you **communicate** with your friends? Do you call, email, or text?

REFLECT Consider how different kinds of music make you feel.

You are going to read about a special kind of music. Discuss the questions with a partner.
1. What kinds of music do you listen to?
2. Do you listen to different kinds of music for different activities? Explain.
3. Can you suggest a kind of music for studying? For doing exercise?

READ

NEW IN THE MUSIC WORLD: VIDEO GAME MUSIC

A PREVIEW Scan the article and answer the questions.

1. What kind of music is the article about? What do you know about this type of music?

2. Look at the photo. Do you want to go to this concert?

B PREDICT Read the sentences. Do you agree? Write Y for *Yes,* N for *No,* or NS for *Not Sure.* Then read the article. Are your opinions still the same?

1. _____ Video games are popular for good reasons.

2. _____ Playing video games is a bad use of time.

3. _____ Music is a very important part of the game experience.

4. _____ Video game music is different from other types of music.

5. _____ Video games are a positive part of culture.

3.2

1 Music is universal[1], but it changes over time along with **culture**. For example, people enjoyed jazz and quiet love songs 50 or 60 years ago. But now, **modern** kinds of music, such as rock, electronic, and hip-hop, are **popular**. One new **type** of music comes from video games. This new music is interesting in three ways.

2 First, video game music (or VGM) works in a different, more interactive[2] way. VGM follows the play of the game. In exciting parts, the music gets faster. During quieter parts, it becomes slower. In difficult parts of the game, players sometimes take a long time. The music often repeats, or loops, for these times. **However**, the music has to stay interesting while looping, so new instruments may join in. Also, players make noises as they play—beeps, **clicks**, and bloops. These noises become part of the soundtrack[3] itself.

3 Second, video game music is an important part of the music business. Many people play video games. They like hearing VGM. Players want to listen to it outside of the game. This makes VGM popular. Many musicians now write and play video game music. This creates[4] jobs. In fact, VGM was worth about $140 billion in 2018.

D GRAMMAR Look at the bold words. Write C for *Count* or NC for *Noncount*.

1. _____ Students often use their phones to look up **information**.

2. _____ Sometimes a bad movie actually has a great **soundtrack**.

3. _____ Quiet music helps some **people** concentrate.

4. _____ **Time** passes more slowly when you are young.

5. _____ **Video games** are popular with my friends.

6. _____ **Rain** makes certain people feel sad.

7. _____ The **concert** starts at 8 p.m. tonight.

GRAMMAR   Quantifiers

Quantifiers tell how much of something there is. We use quantifiers with nouns.
With count nouns:

   *A **few** <u>people</u> in the study listen to background music.*

   ***Some** <u>songs</u> are more modern than other songs.*

   *I don't like **a lot of/many** popular <u>songs</u>.*

With noncount nouns:

   *There's **a little** <u>information</u> about VGM in this article.*

   *I have **some** <u>music</u> on my phone.*

   *There isn't **a lot of** <u>work</u> to do.*

   *We don't have **much** <u>time</u>.*

   *How **much** <u>money</u> do you need?*

E GRAMMAR Choose the correct quantifier or article to complete the paragraph. Choose Ø if the noun does not need a quantifier or article.

A Bad Song

The song *Axel F* is [1]**a / Ø** bad electronic song. [2]**A / Some** Swedish computer character, Crazy Frog, sings it. [3]**Ø / The** music is fast and fun, but it repeats over and over. I have [4]**a few / a little** problems with it. It doesn't have [5]**much / many** words, but it has [6]**a lot of / much** noises, such as beeps and dings. There isn't [7]**Ø / a** story really. It's like a video game. It bothers me when I hear it because it repeats so much. However, it is probably good for [8]**the / Ø** background music when you exercise. *Axel F* may be popular, but overall, it is not a good song.

F Complete the sentences with your ideas.

1. My favorite music has some _____.

2. Music from my culture uses a lot of _____.

3. A good song has many _____.

4. I like a singer with a(n) _____.

5. Musicians need a lot of _____.

6. I listen to music when I have a(n) _____.

G **EDIT** Find and correct six errors with nouns, articles, or quantifiers.

Running to Music

I like to listen to musics when I run. I usually wear the earphones. I play music with a words, and I sing along. Songs make me happy and give me many energy. I run faster when song is fast! An exercise is always better with music. I never run without headphones.

WRITING TIP

A good **title** usually says something about the topic, has key words from the paragraph, and is interesting to the reader. It is also not too long or too short.

PLAN & WRITE

H BRAINSTORM Complete the chart for two types of music that you like or know about. Share your ideas in a group. Then add two more types.

Type of music	Details (instruments, feeling, events, etc.)
mariachi	uses guitars, accordions, trumpets; sounds happy; big bands; plays at weddings

Choose one type of music. Go online and look up information about it. Then choose a song and listen to it.

I OUTLINE Complete the outline for your paragraph about a song.

Title: _____

1. **Topic sentence** (give song name, type of music, and main idea):

   _____

2. **Supporting sentences:**

   a. Who sings/plays/wrote it? _____

   b. Where is it from? _____

   c. What instruments does it use? _____

   d. What words describe it? _____

   e. How does it make you feel? _____

   f. When is a good time to listen to it? _____

3. **Concluding sentence:** _____

J FIRST DRAFT Use the model in activity A and your outline to write a first draft of your paragraph.

K REVISE Use this list as you write your second draft.

☐ Does your topic sentence introduce the main idea of your paragraph?

☐ Do your supporting sentences give more information about the topic?

☐ Does the paragraph have a concluding sentence?

☐ Is there any information that doesn't belong?

L EDIT Use this list as you write your final draft.

☐ Do you use count/noncount nouns, articles, and quantifiers correctly?

☐ Do your subjects and verbs agree?

☐ Do you spell all the words correctly?

☐ Do you use correct capitalization and punctuation?

M FINAL DRAFT Reread your final draft and correct any errors. Then submit it to your teacher.

Listening to music while drawing

REFLECT

A Check (✓) the Reflect activities you can do and the academic skills you can use.

- ☐ consider how you learn
- ☐ write a song or rhyme to remember words
- ☐ consider how different kinds of music make you feel
- ☐ analyze a type of music
- ☐ write a paragraph about a song

- ☐ identify supporting sentences and details
- ☐ write supporting sentences
- ☐ count and noncount nouns
- ☐ quantifiers
- ☐ analyze information

B Check (✓) the vocabulary words from the unit that you know. Circle words you still need to practice. Add any other words that you learned.

NOUN	VERB	ADJECTIVE	ADVERB & OTHER
background	communicate	certain	actually
click	concentrate	modern	however
culture	repeat	noisy	
experience	solve	popular	
memory		quiet	
sound		useful	
type			
volume			

C Reflect on the ideas in the unit as you answer these questions.

1. Which part of the unit did you enjoy the most? Explain.

_____

_____

2. What ideas or skills in this unit will be most useful to you in the future?

_____

_____

Citizen scientists replant coral in Moorea, French Polynesia.

IN THIS UNIT

▶ Think about how you can get involved

▶ Connect ideas about citizen science

▶ Think about why we explore

▶ Take steps to reach a goal

▶ Write a paragraph about a citizen science project

SKILLS

READING
Guess meaning from context

WRITING
Write about steps in a process

GRAMMAR
Simple past

CRITICAL THINKING
Weigh advantages and disadvantages

CONNECT TO THE TOPIC

1. Why do you think the men are replanting the coral?

2. What do you think you need to be a scientist?

WATCH

WHAT IS CITIZEN SCIENCE?

Citizen scientists look at a guide book to identify plants.

A These words will help you understand the video. Match the words with their definitions. Note that some of the words are similar in meaning.

1. _____ naturalist
2. _____ citizen
3. _____ conservationist
4. _____ volunteer
5. _____ biodiversity

a. a member of a country, state, or city
b. a person who works but doesn't get money
c. a person who works to help plants and animals
d. a variety of plants and animals
e. a person who studies plants and animals

B Watch the video. Put the ideas in the order you hear them. ▶ 4.1

a. _____ Volunteers get some training, such as ID guides or workshops.

b. _____ Citizen science helps people learn and become excited about nature.

c. _____ In the spring, flowers and insects come out.

d. _____ Citizen science saves money.

e. _____ Citizen scientists are volunteers who collect data, or information.

f. _____ Some citizen scientists may teach at a university, but others have less experience.

PREPARE TO READ

A VOCABULARY Read the sentences. Write the words in **bold** next to their definitions.

    a. You don't have to buy the book. It is **available** in the library and online.

    b. Teachers usually **collect** their students' homework. They look at it after class.

    c. Mia has a **diary**. She tries to write a few sentences every day.

    d. I'm very short. That is a **disadvantage** when I play basketball.

    e. Most people can't work for **free**. They need money to pay for things.

    f. I love to be out in **nature**. I feel better when I'm outside with trees and grass.

    g. My uncle is a **professional** botanist. His job is to study plants.

    h. Did someone take your bag? You should **report** it to the police.

    i. This **task** is very simple. Anyone can do it.

    j. The movie looks really good. **Unfortunately**, we're busy tonight and can't go.

1. _____ (n) something that gets in the way; a problem

2. _____ (v) to bring together

3. _____ (adj) without cost or payment

4. _____ (v) to describe or tell about something

5. _____ (adj) able to use; ready to get

6. _____ (n) the world not made by humans; plants and animals

7. _____ (n) a small job; a chore

8. _____ (adj) relating to work that needs special training

9. _____ (adv) sadly; without luck

10. _____ (n) personal writing about daily activities or events

REFLECT Think about how you can get involved.

You are going to read more about citizen science. Answer the questions, and then discuss with a group.

1. What area of science interests you?

2. What skills do you have that might make you a good citizen scientist?

3. How can you learn more about citizen science projects in the area that interests you?

READ

A PREDICT As you learned from the video, a *citizen scientist* is a person who helps with scientific work. In what ways do you think they can help? Check your ideas after you read.

B MAIN IDEAS Read the sentences. Write T for *True,* F for *False,* or NG for *Not Given.*

1. _____ Citizen science uses mostly professional scientists.

2. _____ Using volunteers has good points and bad points.

3. _____ The idea of normal people doing research is new.

4. _____ Most citizen science projects count animals.

5. _____ Researchers follow certain steps in each project.

C MAIN IDEAS The article has six paragraphs. Match the paragraph number to each topic.

a. _____ Steps in a citizen science project

b. _____ Citizen science in the past

c. _____ Types of citizen science projects now

d. _____ The Great Backyard Bird Count

e. _____ Concluding ideas about citizen science

f. _____ Advantages and disadvantages of citizen science

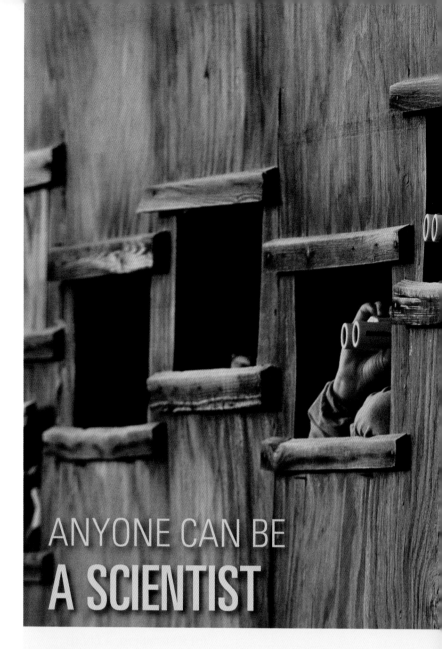

ANYONE CAN BE A SCIENTIST

🎧 4.1

1   On one weekend every February, 160,000 people from around the world help in the Great Backyard Bird Count. You don't need to be a **professional** birdwatcher. You just need 15 minutes, an interest in birds, and a notebook. In a bird count, people write down the number of birds they see. This is an example of a popular form of research: citizen science.

2   Citizen science uses a lot of volunteers. Citizens, or normal people, **collect** information for research. Citizen science has some important advantages. Thousands of people from all over the world help. Volunteers work for **free**, so it is not expensive. And the volunteers learn new skills. There are also some **disadvantages**. **Unfortunately**, volunteers make mistakes

Birdwatchers at the Lillian Annette Rowe Sanctuary, Platte River, Nebraska, USA.

sometimes. Or a project can miss information because there aren't enough volunteers.

3   The term "citizen science" is new, but this kind of research is very old. Long ago, people wrote about events in **nature**, like storms. For example, 2,000 years ago, Chinese farmers had a problem with <u>locusts</u>, large flying insects. The insects destroyed their <u>crops</u>, so the farmers had no food. The farmers took notes on the years with locusts. This helped them plan better.

4   Now, there are different kinds of citizen science projects. Many projects are **available** online. Volunteers do a lot of the work at home. For example, people can play games on their phones to identify animals. Or volunteers can type up notes from the **diaries** of famous artists. Other projects are in the field. For

instance, people can go outside with others and identify flowers or count insects.

5   There are several steps in a citizen science project. First, researchers decide on a problem (Why are there fewer birds?). Then they identify their goals. Next, they decide on **tasks** for volunteers. Researchers make the work simple and <u>clear</u> (Count the birds in each photo.). After that, they find volunteers. During the project, volunteers collect information. The researchers analyze it. Finally, the researchers **report** on the project.

6   Citizen science has come a long way in a few thousand years. It began with farmers who kept records of important events in nature. Today, researchers use it to get help on their projects. With citizen science, anyone can be a scientist.

READING SKILL Guess meaning from context

You can guess the meaning of an unfamiliar, or new, word from the **context**. Read the words and sentences around the unfamiliar word to understand what it means.

In a bird **count**, _people write down the number of birds they see_.

The word _count_ probably means "a total number."

Sometimes the definition is in the sentence, between commas, parentheses, or dashes.

Citizens, _or normal people_, collect information for research.

The word _citizens_ in this context probably means "normal people."

D APPLY Use the context to guess the meaning of the <u>underlined</u> words in the article.

1. In paragraph 3, a _locust_ is a kind of _____.

   a. insect   b. food   c. farmer

2. In paragraph 3, the word _crop_ means _____.

   a. a lot of rain   b. an area of land   c. plants grown for food

3. In paragraph 5, the word _clear_ could be changed to _____.

   a. easy to understand   b. light   c. hard to understand

E DETAILS Match the two sentence parts.

1. _____ One advantage of citizen science is   a. deciding on a problem.

2. _____ One disadvantage is   b. destroy crops.

3. _____ Locusts hurt farmers because they   c. researchers report on the project.

4. _____ In some projects, volunteers identify   d. animals or flowers.

5. _____ The first step in a project is   e. simple and clear.

6. _____ The work in a project needs to be   f. it's not expensive.

7. _____ In the last step of a project,   g. people make mistakes.

REFLECT   Connect ideas about citizen science.

Think about the video and the article. Discuss the questions with a partner.

1. What ideas are in both the video and the article?

2. Is the research of citizen scientists as good as the work of trained scientists? Explain.

3. Citizen science helps researchers. How can it help volunteers?

PREPARE TO READ

A VOCABULARY Read the sentences. Choose the definitions for the words in **bold**.

a. short (adj)

b. opinion about what to do (n)

c. to make sure something is correct or OK (v)

d. people you work with (n)

1. _____ Here's some **advice** for students: Study hard and do your homework.

2. _____ We need to write a **brief** description—only a few sentences.

3. _____ Students should **check** their homework before they give it to their teacher.

4. _____ My **colleagues** in the office usually arrive early.

e. definitely; completely (adv)

f. things needed for work (n)

g. to find; to learn about (v)

5. _____ How do you **discover** great new restaurants? Do you ask friends?

6. _____ Scientists use **equipment** such as telescopes and special cameras.

7. _____ How many birds did you see **exactly**? Did you see 42, or 43?

h. repeated things, such as shapes or colors (n)

i. almost (adv)

j. to become a member of (v)

8. _____ I want to **join** a hiking club.

9. _____ The meeting is **nearly** over. Can you wait a few more minutes?

10. _____ She studies the **patterns** in nature and uses them in her art.

B PERSONALIZE Think about the questions. Then share your thoughts with a partner.

1. You are meeting some new **colleagues** at work. Give a **brief** description of yourself.

2. What **advice** can you give to someone who wants to learn English?

3. Are you a member of a club? If so, what **exactly** do you do in the club?

REFLECT Think about why we explore.

You are going to read about the discovery of a planet. Why do scientists want to explore and what equipment do they use? Discuss your ideas in a group. Take notes below.

Reasons to explore	Equipment scientists use

READ

A PREVIEW Look at the photos and read the captions. Scan the article. What do you know about this topic? What do you want to learn about this topic?

B MAIN IDEAS Read the article and check (✓) the four main ideas.

1. _____ Wolf learned how to find a planet as a volunteer with a citizen science project.

2. _____ Planet Hunters volunteers discover many new planets.

3. _____ Student interns like Wolf often get into good colleges.

4. _____ Wolf was an intern with NASA.

5. _____ Wolf used his experience as a volunteer to discover a planet.

6. _____ Other scientists helped and made sure the work was correct.

7. _____ Many newspapers reported on Wolf's planet.

READING TIP

To help you understand and remember the information you read, stop after each paragraph and ask: *What is this about?*

Wolf Cukier, teen scientist

TEEN DISCOVERS A PLANET

🎧 4.2

1 Some people sit through meetings on the first few days of a new job, but one teen **discovered** a planet[1]—on his third day at the Goddard Space Flight Center in Greenbelt, Maryland, USA. How did 17-year-old Wolf Cukier do this?

2 Before his work at Goddard, Wolf was a volunteer with Planet Hunters. Planet Hunters is a citizen science project. It hunts, or looks, for new planets. It's easy to work on this project. Volunteers complete a **brief** training online. Then they look at <u>images</u> of stars[2] from a satellite[3]. They look for changes in **patterns** of light. When a planet moves in front of a star, the star becomes darker. Volunteers report the changes they see. Because of this volunteer work, Wolf knew about finding planets.

High school student Wolf Cukier helped scientists discover this exoplanet.

3   Then Wolf got an <u>internship</u> through his school. Internships are a good way to learn about a job. Interns often don't get paid, but they get a lot of experience. Wolf's internship was at the Goddard Space Flight Center. It is part of the National Air and Space Administration (NASA). Goddard sends **equipment**, including satellites, into space for research.

4   As an intern, Wolf helped scientist Veselin Kostov. After only three days, Wolf discovered a planet. The planet is **nearly** seven times larger than Earth. It has two stars. Wolf compared it to the planet Tatooine from *Star Wars*.

5   What did Wolf do **exactly**? He knew how to look for a planet from Planet Hunters. At his internship, he saw something unusual on a picture. He told Kostov. They both did more research. Then they worked with **colleagues** to <u>confirm</u> the discovery. It took about three months to **check** that the information was correct. Wolf wrote a paper about his work with the other scientists.

6   Wolf thinks other kids can be scientists, too. He gives this **advice**: "Just start doing science: tinker with[4] stuff, or do a project." Or **join** a school science team and get an internship like he did. His high school experience and volunteer work led Wolf to his big discovery. What will Wolf do on his next summer vacation? The possibilities are endless.

---

[1]**planet** (n) an object in space that moves around a sun

[2]**star** (n) a ball of burning gases in the sky, such as the sun

[3]**satellite** (n) a piece of equipment sent into space that moves around a planet, usually to collect information

[4]**tinker with** (v phr) to make small changes to improve something

C Use the context to guess the meaning of the underlined words in the article.

1. In paragraph 2, what does *image* probably mean?

   a. a picture   b. a piece   c. a story

2. In paragraph 3, what do people with an *internship* do?

   a. make a lot of money   b. take online classes   c. work to get experience

3. In paragraph 5, what does *confirm* probably mean?

   a. to report on something   b. to show that something is false   c. to check that something is correct

D DETAILS Answer the questions. Write one to three words.

1. What was the name of Cukier's citizen science project? _____

2. Volunteers look at images. What do they look for changes in? _____

3. Wolf helped a scientist. What was his name? _____

4. How many stars does the planet Wolf discovered have? _____

5. How long did it take to make sure it was a planet? _____

CRITICAL THINKING   **Weigh advantages and disadvantages**

Actions often have both advantages and disadvantages. When you need to decide something, list the ways it improves your life and the ways it could hurt or be a problem. Which list is longer? Use this information to make a decision.

E APPLY Which is right for you? Work with a partner to complete the chart.

	Advantages	Disadvantages
Volunteer work		
Internships		

REFLECT   Take steps to reach a goal.

Answer the questions. Then discuss with a partner.

1. What is a goal that you have?

2. What volunteer work or internships can help you reach this goal?

3. What other steps can you take to reach your goal?

WRITE

Write a paragraph about a citizen science project.

You are going to write a paragraph about a project that a citizen scientist did. Use the ideas, vocabulary, and skills from the unit.

A MODEL Read the paragraph. Circle the project name. Underline the purpose of the project.

SquirrelMapper

I was a volunteer on a project called SquirrelMapper. Gray squirrels are more common than black ones. Scientists want to know the reason. I followed clear steps. First, I read the directions on the website. Then I looked at pictures of squirrels. I clicked on the number of squirrels in each picture, and I clicked on the color of the squirrels. I identified squirrels in 10 photos. Finally, I read the online discussion. I learned interesting facts about squirrels by following these steps.

B ANALYZE THE MODEL Complete the outline of the model paragraph.

1. **Topic sentence** (what you did): _____

2. **Supporting sentences:**

   a. Purpose of project: _____

   b. Step 1: _____

   c. Step 2: _____

   d. Step 3: _____

   e. Step 4: _____

3. **Concluding sentence** (what you learned): _____

WRITING SKILL Write about steps in a process

When you write about several different **steps** in a process, use **time order words**, or transitions. These words tell the reader the order that steps or events happen.

first   second   next   then   after that   later   finally

Use time order words at the beginning of a sentence. Use a comma after the words, except *then*.

C APPLY Choose the correct words to complete the paragraph.

Mountain Watch

I chose to help Mountain Watch. The project studies changes in weather through photos. [1]**First, / Then** I read the instructions on the website. [2]**Finally, / Next,** I got an app for my phone. [3]**Second, / After that,** I went hiking on Grandfather Mountain and took 50 pictures of flowers. [4]**Then / Finally,** I put the photos on the website. [5]**First, / Finally,** I checked the website to find the names of the flowers. On the project, I learned about flowers and weather changes.

D Read the sentences about a citizen science project the writer did. Put the sentences in order. Then rewrite them as a paragraph on a separate piece of paper.

Community Traffic Project

a. _____ My street is very busy, and I think it needs a traffic light.

b. _____ First, I took my chair and phone outside from 8 a.m. to 9 a.m.

c. __1__ In my science project, I studied the traffic on my street.

d. _____ I did the same thing every day for a week.

e. _____ Finally, I emailed someone in town hall with the information.

f. _____ Then I counted the number of cars and took notes on my phone.

g. _____ After that, I wrote a report about the week.

h. _____ I learned to use a science project to help my community.

GRAMMAR Simple past

We use the **simple past** to talk about past events and completed actions.

*We **worked** on the project yesterday.*

We can also use the simple past to talk about repeated past actions.

*The volunteer **helped** exactly <u>seven times</u> last year.*

We often use the simple past with time words such as *two days/weeks/years ago, last week/month/summer,* and *yesterday.*

*I **watched** birds for 15 minutes every day <u>last February</u>.*

Regular verbs end in *-ed.*

add *-ed: report* → *report**ed***   change *y* to *i*, add *-ed: study* → *stud**ied***

add *-d: decide* → *decide**d***   double consonant, add *-ed: stop* → *stop**ped***

Many common verbs have irregular past forms.

be → *was/were*   *do* → *did*   *go* → *went*   *have* → *had*   *see* → *saw*   *write* → *wrote*

Use *did not (didn't)* + base form to make negative statements.

*She **didn't see** any squirrels. The interns **didn't find** a lot of information.*

E GRAMMAR Write the simple past of the verbs.

1. add _____

2. check _____

3. collect _____

4. count _____

5. drive _____

6. find _____

7. get _____

8. go _____

9. have _____

10. know _____

11. learn _____

12. measure _____

13. plan _____

14. put _____

15. read _____

16. report _____

17. see _____

18. study _____

19. take _____

20. write _____

F GRAMMAR Complete the sentences with the simple past of the verbs.

1. In the past, farmers _____ (be) citizen scientists.

2. The researchers _____ (contact) the volunteers.

3. They _____ (communicate) nearly every day last week.

4. I _____ (not, agree) with Sarah about the kind of bird.

5. In the project last month, people _____ (solve) simple math problems.

6. The scientists _____ (stop) the research two years ago.

7. My colleagues _____ (worry) about the animals.

8. The team _____ (not, do) any research on planets.

G EDIT Read the paragraph. Find and correct five errors with the simple past.

Great Backyard Bird Count

I helped with the Great Backyard Bird Count (GBBC) last year. In the GBBC project, researchers studied the flight patterns of birds. First, I read about the project on the website. Then last February, I go outside for 15 minutes. I saw eight different kinds of birds. I count the number of each kind. I wrote the number down. Next, I went online, and I create an account. I clicked on the place on a map. After that, I added my list of birds. I learned a lot about the birds in my own backyard. I didn't knew there were so many!

Every year 160,000 people help with the Great Backyard Bird Count.

PLAN & WRITE

H PLAN Look at a student's plan for a citizen scientist project. Put the steps in the correct order. Match the steps to the correct photos.

Citizen Science Project: Mosquito Mapper
Purpose: Help scientists understand dangers from mosquitoes

Steps:

a. Remove the place where mosquitoes live.

b. Get an app to record the research.

c. Find and photograph a place where mosquitoes live.

d. Photograph and identify young mosquitoes.

Step 1 _____

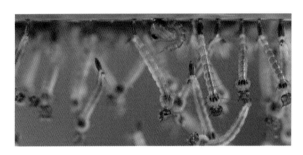

Step 3 _____

Step 2 _____

Step 4 _____

I OUTLINE Complete the outline.

1. **Topic sentence** (what the student did): _____

2. **Supporting sentences:**

   a. Purpose of project: _____

   b. Step 1: _____

   c. Step 2: _____

   d. Step 3: _____

   e. Step 4: _____

3. **Concluding sentence** (what the student learned): _____

J FIRST DRAFT Use the model in activity A and your outline to write a first draft of your paragraph.

K REVISE Use this list as you write your second draft.

☐ Does your topic sentence identify the science project?

☐ Do you give the purpose of the research?

☐ Do you list the steps you followed?

☐ Do you use time order words to organize the steps?

☐ Does the paragraph have a concluding sentence?

☐ Is there any information that doesn't belong?

> **WRITING TIP**
>
> Remember to **indent**, or add a space before, the first sentence of each paragraph. Indenting shows the reader that a new paragraph is beginning.

L EDIT Use this list as you write your final draft.

☐ Do you use the simple past correctly?

☐ Do your subjects and verbs agree?

☐ Do you spell all the words correctly?

☐ Do you use correct capitalization and punctuation?

M FINAL DRAFT Reread your final draft and correct any errors. Then submit it to your teacher.

Some citizen science projects, such as Mountain Watch, ask volunteers to photograph and identify flowers.

REFLECT

A Check (✓) the Reflect activities you can do and the academic skills you can use.

☐ think about how you can get involved

☐ connect ideas about citizen science

☐ think about why we explore

☐ take steps to reach a goal

☐ write a paragraph about a citizen science project

☐ guess meaning from context

☐ write about steps in a process

☐ simple past

☐ weigh advantages and disadvantages

B Check (✓) the vocabulary words from the unit that you know. Circle words you still need to practice. Add any other words that you learned.

NOUN	VERB	ADJECTIVE	ADVERB & OTHER
advice	check	available	exactly
colleague	collect	brief	nearly
diary	discover	free	unfortunately
disadvantage	join	professional	
equipment	report		
nature			
pattern			
task			

C Reflect on the ideas in the unit as you answer these questions.

1. Did this unit change the way you think about science?

   _____

   _____

2. What ideas and skills in this unit will be most useful to you in the future?

   _____

   _____

FOOD
ADVERTISING

IN THIS UNIT

▶ Think about your food buying habits

▶ Understand how food labels affect you

▶ Think critically about food choices

▶ Analyze food labels

▶ Write a paragraph about food

SKILLS

READING
Identify facts and opinions

WRITING
Write concluding sentences

GRAMMAR
Modals for suggestions and advice

CRITICAL THINKING
Evaluate writers' claims

A food stylist uses a paint brush to make these tacos look good.

CONNECT TO THE TOPIC

1. What do you think a food stylist does? Is it an interesting job?

2. Where do you usually buy your food? Why?

WATCH

MAKING FOOD LOOK GOOD

A ACTIVATE Which of these do you eat or drink? Discuss with a partner.

apple	cheese	fish	pizza	strawberry
banana	chicken	ice cream	rice	tea
bread	chocolate	lemon	shrimp	tomato
carrot	coffee	pasta	soda	water

B Watch the video. Check (✓) the things in activity A that you see. ▶ 5.1

C Watch again. Read the sentences. Write T for *True,* F for *False,* or NG for *Not Given.* ▶ 5.1

1. _____ In ads, companies make food move quickly so it will look exciting.

2. _____ A food stylist makes the food look good.

3. _____ Food stylists get a lot of money for their work.

4. _____ You can't see if the food is hot or cold in an ad.

5. _____ Advertisements sometimes show food as art.

D Answer the questions in a group.

1. Do you think ads tell the truth about food? Explain.

2. A good food ad makes you want to eat, whether you're hungry or not. Do you want to eat the foods in the video? Explain.

PREPARE TO READ

A VOCABULARY Complete the sentences with the correct words.

attract (v)	customer (n)	give up (v phr)	label (n)	order (v)
convince (v)	encourage (v)	instead (adv)	menu (n)	section (n)

1. The biology book is in the science _____ of the library.

2. People with heart disease should _____ or stop eating foods with a lot of fat.

3. The _____ on the back of the box tells you the amount of sugar.

4. The _____ has five sandwiches, two kinds of pasta, and three salads.

5. Doctors _____ people to eat healthy foods, but people don't always listen.

6. Flowers _____ birds and bees.

7. I usually _____ chicken and rice for lunch at the restaurant.

8. Don't eat so much candy. You should eat fruit and vegetables _____.

9. The waiter brought the wrong food to the _____.

10. A good food ad can _____ people that they want to eat that food.

B PERSONALIZE Answer the questions.

1. What **attracts** you to certain foods?_____

2. Do you read the **labels** on your food? Explain.

_____

3. Do you usually **order** the same thing from a **menu**, or something different? Why?

_____

REFLECT   Think about your food buying habits.

You are going to read about how companies can influence what we eat. How do you decide on which food to buy or order? Rank the ideas below (1 = most important, 6 = least important). Then compare with a partner.

_____ Is it good for the environment?   _____ Is it expensive?

_____ Is it healthy for me?   _____ Does it look good?

_____ Does it taste good?   _____ Does the ad or menu convince me?

READ

DELICIOUS VEGAN BURGERS

100% vegan!

Low-fat! Meat-free!

Light & healthy!

Juicy & delicious!

Find us in the vegetarian section of your favorite grocery store

The Vegan Food Company

A PREDICT Choose the correct words to complete your predictions. Then read and check your answers.

1. The labels *vegan* and *vegetarian* **are / are not** popular with people who eat meat.

2. Words such as *light* or *fat-free* **help / don't help** to sell food.

3. People **like / don't like** to know where food comes from.

WHAT'S IN A NAME? `1.51`

1   Research shows we should eat more plants and less meat to improve our health and the environment. Daniel Vennard works at the World Resources Institute (WRI). WRI tries to solve problems with food, energy, water, and cities. Vennard's job is to **convince** meat-eaters to eat less meat. It's not easy. Why? A juicy burger just sounds more delicious than healthy broccoli. To reach the goal, Vennard says we have to change the words we use.

2   A new report from WRI discusses different ways to describe food from plants. Some descriptions don't work at all. People who eat meat dislike **labels** with the words *vegan*[1] or *vegetarian*[2]. In one study, vegetarian food is in a special **section** of the **menu**. People were 56 percent less likely to **order** those food items. The same food items in a list with all the meat dishes were much more popular. Also, when labels have the words *no, low, light,* or *free,* fewer people buy them. In a British study, people didn't buy many "meat-free sausages[3]." However, they bought the same sausages with the words "spiced veggie sausages." It seems that people don't want to **give** anything **up**.

3   The report also discusses successful ways to describe plant-based food. First, it helps to talk about where the food comes from. The restaurant Panera offered "low-fat vegetarian black bean soup." Not many people ordered it. When they changed the name to "Cuban black bean soup," they sold 13 percent more. Another way to sell more food is to describe its taste, for example, *sweet* or *spicy*. When the adjectives sound delicious, people will buy the food. Finally, companies can use words about color and texture[4] to sell more food. **Customers** like words such as *bright, colorful,* and *crisp.*

4   Vennard wants companies, organizations, and restaurants to help the environment and improve health. These businesses can **encourage** people to eat less meat and more vegetables and fruit **instead**. To sell more food from plants, they should use language that **attracts** customers. They can talk about taste, color, and texture if they want to change minds. After all, food should be enjoyable.

---

[1]**vegan** (adj) not made from meat or any animal products
[2]**vegetarian** (adj) not made from meat
[3]**sausage** (n) chopped meat and spices in a long shape
[4]**texture** (n) the way that something feels

B MAIN IDEAS Read the sentences. Write T for *True* or F for *False.*

1. _____ People should eat less meat to improve their health and help the environment.

2. _____ People prefer words like *no* and *low* on food labels.

3. _____ People buy more food when companies talk about countries, taste, and color.

4. _____ Changing words can help change people's minds about food.

C MAIN IDEAS Work with a partner. Look at the ad. Which words don't work, according to the article? Put a line through them. Which ones do? Circle them.

READING SKILL Identify facts and opinions

As you read, it is important to recognize the difference between facts and opinions. A **fact** is something most people agree is true. We can usually check a fact. Facts include:

- ▶ numbers — *Water boils at 100 degrees Celsius.*
- ▶ dates — *On January 1, people in South Korea often eat soup.*
- ▶ names — *Injera is a common food in Ethiopia.*

An **opinion** is something a person thinks or believes. Other people may agree or disagree. Opinions often include:

- ▶ adjectives, such as *best, beautiful, wonderful, terrible,* and *interesting.*
  Water is the best drink to have at breakfast.
- ▶ modals or other expressions, such as *should, can, might, have to,* and *must.*
  You should eat more soup.
- ▶ introductory phrases, such as *I think, I believe,* and *in my opinion.*
  I think injera tastes delicious.

D DETAILS Complete the sentences from the article with one to three words or numbers. Then write F for *Fact* or O for *Opinion.*

1. _____ Daniel Vennard works at the _____.

2. _____ A juicy burger just sounds more _____ than healthy broccoli.

3. _____ People were _____ percent less likely to order those food items.

4. _____ In _____, people didn't buy many "meat-free sausages."

5. _____ When they changed the name to "Cuban black bean soup," they sold _____ percent more.

6. _____ To sell more food from plants, they _____ language that attracts customers.

7. _____ After all, food _____ enjoyable.

REFLECT Understand how food labels affect you.

Answer the questions. Then discuss with a partner.

1. Do you buy food with these words on the label: *vegan/vegetarian, light, low,* and *free?* Explain.

_____

2. What adjectives make you want to try a new food? Why?

_____

PREPARE TO READ

A VOCABULARY Write the words in **bold** next to their definitions.

   a. Put the chicken in the hot pan. Watch it **carefully**.

   b. I have a healthy **diet**. I eat a lot of fruit and vegetables.

   c. **Fast food**, like hamburgers and French fries, isn't very good for your health.

   d. My breakfast **includes** coffee, milk, bread, and fruit.

   e. An apple is **natural**, but soda is not.

   f. Some ads have a **negative** effect on us. We don't want to buy the product.

   g. We have two **options**. We can eat out at a restaurant, or stay home and cook.

   h. That store sells a lot of Italian food **products**. I bought pasta there.

   i. When customers want to **select** healthy foods, they should read the labels.

   j. I like to drink **whole** milk. It tastes better than low-fat milk.

1. _____ (n) things you can choose

2. _____ (v) to have as part of a group

3. _____ (adv) in a way to avoid getting hurt or making a mistake

4. _____ (adj) not positive; not good

5. _____ (v) to choose from a group of similar things

6. _____ (adj) all of; entire; complete

7. _____ (n) the food a person or animal usually eats

8. _____ (adj) existing in nature; not made by people

9. _____ (n) things that are made (usually in a factory) and sold

10. _____ (n) food that is cooked and eaten quickly in a restaurant

---

REFLECT Think critically about food choices.

You are going to read about how to make good food choices. Answer the questions. Then discuss with a partner.

1. What do you think a healthy diet should include?

_____

2. Are some food products more natural than others? What are their benefits?

_____

3. Are there healthy options at a fast food restaurant? Do you select them? Explain.

_____

READ

Customers at a market in São Paulo, Brazil, try the fruit to decide what to buy.

A PREVIEW Answer the questions.

1. Look at the title, photo, and caption. How does the photo connect to the article?

2. Read the first sentence of each paragraph. What topics are the same as the ones in the reading *What's in a Name?*

READING TIP

Writers often use questions to focus on the topic of a paragraph. When you read, notice questions in the text and read to find the answers.

DECISIONS, DECISIONS 🎧 5.2

1   Veggie burgers as juicy as beef? Tofu as spicy as sausage? Can fake[1] meat be delicious and healthy, too? Maybe not. We all know that vegetables and other **whole** foods are part of a healthy **diet**, but some plant-based foods may actually be unhealthy. Before you decide whether to eat real or fake meat, there are some important points to consider.

2   Some people are influenced by[2] a "health halo." What is a "health halo"? When a food has one positive thing or benefit, people think it has many. For example, customers may see *low fat* on a cup of yogurt. They **select** the yogurt because they think it is healthy, but it may have 47 grams of sugar! A health halo helps companies. Customers may think that a restaurant with a few healthy **options** on the menu has healthier food in general.

3   This health halo often applies to vegan or vegetarian food. But many of these foods are not very healthy at all. Let's look at veggie burgers. Companies usually add salt and unnatural ingredients to make the vegetables taste and feel more like meat. For example, Burger King®'s plant-based Impossible™ Whopper® has more salt than their beef Whopper®. Food made in a factory, or processed food, is usually less healthy than more **natural**, or whole, food.

4   Should we have a **negative** opinion of meat? There are some good reasons to have less meat in our diets. Eating a lot of beef can be bad for our hearts. However, meat is not the only problem. People eat a lot of **fast food**. That's bad for our hearts, too. Also, meat is a good source of protein[3] and some nutrients. People need both for good health, and it's hard to get enough from plant-based foods alone. Raising beef uses a lot of water and land. But other animal **products**, such as chicken, fish, and cheese, use much less. And some fake meat products are as bad for the environment as chicken.

5   In general, people don't like to be told what to do. We want to make our own decisions about our food. A vegetarian diet may be a good choice for some people, but it's more important to choose a diet that **includes** vegetables, fruit, protein, and whole grains such as rice, wheat, and corn. Everyone must read labels **carefully** to make sure what they are eating is really healthy.

---

[1]**fake** (adj) not real; not natural

[2]**be influenced by** (v phr) to act a certain way because of something

[3]**protein** (n) something in food like fish, meat, and eggs that helps people and animals grow and be healthy

---

B MAIN IDEAS The article has five paragraphs. Match the paragraph number to each main idea.

1. _____ It's important to read labels when you select your food.

2. _____ Many vegan and vegetarian foods are not as healthy as you think.

3. _____ A health halo makes you believe food with one healthy thing has many.

4. _____ Fake meat, like veggie burgers, may not be healthy.

5. _____ Meat can be part of a healthy diet.

C APPLY Read the sentences. Write F for *Fact* or O for *Opinion.*

1. _____ Can fake meat be delicious and healthy, too? Maybe not.

2. _____ Some yogurt has 47 grams of sugar.

3. _____ Burger King®'s plant-based Impossible™ Whopper® has more salt than their beef Whopper®.

4. _____ There are some good reasons to have less meat in our diets.

D DETAILS Complete the sentences with the correct information.

companies	fish	protein
fast food	labels	natural food

1. A health halo helps _____.

2. Processed food is not as healthy as _____.

3. Eating too much beef and _____ can be bad for our hearts.

4. People need _____ and nutrients for good health.

5. Chicken and _____ are better for the environment than beef.

6. Information on _____ can help us choose healthy food.

CRITICAL THINKING Evaluate writers' claims

When writers express opinions, they often make **claims**, or say something is true. Strong claims have facts to support them. When you read, check whether the writer gives facts to support his or her claims.

Claim: *Some yogurt is unhealthy.*
Support: *For example, some yogurts have 47 grams of sugar.*

E APPLY Evaluate the writers' claims in the articles in this unit. Find two claims from each writer and look for support. Who do you think has stronger claims? Compare your ideas with a partner.

REFLECT Analyze food labels.

Choose a food product at home, online, or at the supermarket. Read its nutrition label. Answer the questions. Then discuss with a partner.

1. What is your food product?

2. What does the label tell you about the food?

3. What words can you use to describe the food?

WRITE

UNIT TASK Write a paragraph about food.

> You are going to write a paragraph about food choices or food ads. You will give an opinion and support it with reasons. Use the ideas, vocabulary, and skills from the unit.

A MODEL Read the paragraph. Underline the topic sentence.

Food Labels

Customers should read labels before they buy a food product. Labels have important information about nutrients. They include information such as how many grams of fat, sugar, and protein are in the food. Labels also tell you about the kind of food in the product. For example, you can look for unnatural, processed ingredients or natural ingredients, such as whole grains. To sum up, I think labels give very helpful information to customers.

B ANALYZE THE MODEL Complete the outline of the paragraph.

Topic sentence:

Supporting idea 1:	**Supporting idea 2:**
Detail(s):	**Detail(s):**

Concluding sentence:

WRITING SKILL Write concluding sentences

The last sentence in a paragraph is usually the **concluding sentence**. The concluding sentence is important because it tells the reader you are finished presenting your idea. It can:

▸ say the main idea again in different words
▸ give the writer's opinion
▸ make a suggestion

It may begin with phrases such as *in conclusion, in summary, in short,* or *to sum up.*

C APPLY Reread the topic sentence and the concluding sentence in the model paragraph. What ideas are in both? Look for repeated words.

_____

_____

D APPLY Read the topic sentences. Choose the best concluding sentence.

1. The ad for the *Impossible Burger* is very successful.

    a. The *Impossible Burger* ad makes me want to try it.

    b. The *Impossible Burger* has less fat than a regular burger.

2. Food companies should show real food in ads and not edit the photos to make the food look better.

    a. Beautiful photos in ads sell food, but companies should tell the truth about their products.

    b. Most food ads use beautiful pictures because people like to look at them, and because they sell more food that way.

3. In my opinion, people shouldn't completely give up food they enjoy.

    a. For example, steak is one of my favorite foods, and I want to eat it sometimes.

    b. In short, giving up food you enjoy doesn't solve problems, but it may create some.

E APPLY Reread the model paragraph. Write a different concluding sentence.

_____

_____

GRAMMAR Modals for suggestions and advice

We use **modals** to make suggestions and give advice. Modals are followed by the base form of the verb. Modals don't change form.

> You **can/could/might eat** more fruit and vegetables. (less strong)
>
> People **shouldn't eat** fake meat. They **should eat** natural foods. (stronger)
>
> We **must eat** less meat to help the environment. We **must not hurt** our planet. (very strong)

We don't usually use a contraction for *must not.*

F GRAMMAR Complete the sentences with verb phrases from the box.

can ask	might convince	must not eat	should tell
could add	must include	should read	shouldn't order

1. People with heart disease _____ a lot of salt.

2. The food company _____ some words about taste or color to the label.

3. Food labels _____ a list of all the ingredients.

4. Beautiful photos _____ more people to buy the food.

5. Customers _____ labels carefully.

6. We _____ two pizzas. It's too much food.

7. Companies _____ the truth in ads. False statements are bad for business.

8. You _____ your doctor about the best diet for you.

G GRAMMAR Choose the correct modals to complete the sentences. Discuss your answers with a partner.

1. A customer **should / must** ask the waiter about food on the menu.
2. Restaurants **shouldn't / must** tell their customers the price of menu items.
3. Fish makes some people very sick. They **might not / must not** eat it.
4. Parents **must not / can** encourage their children to try new vegetables.
5. A good ad **should / shouldn't** attract attention. It **can / shouldn't** be boring.

H GRAMMAR Answer the questions with modals.

1. What can people do to make better decisions about food shopping?

   _____

2. What should you remember when you are ordering food?

   _____

3. Is there anything people must or must not do when they shop for food?

   _____

I EDIT Read the paragraph. Find and correct three errors with modals.

The Best TV Commercials

A successful TV commercial must makes people feel good. One of the best TV commercials of all time was a Coke ad. In the 1971 ad, many young people sang a song about peace and love. It showed that people could come together and be kind. Of course, it also showed we should to drink Coke. In conclusion, I think every company should studying great commercials if they want to sell a lot of products.

A famous Coca-Cola® ad from 1971

PLAN & WRITE

J BRAINSTORM Read Topic A and Topic B below. Then complete the charts with these ideas or your own.

A plant-based diet is better for the environment.	Companies need to make money.
It's the customers' job to stay healthy.	It doesn't kill animals.
It may encourage unhealthy eating.	Meat has protein.
Meat is delicious.	It isn't honest.

Topic A: People should eat less meat.	
Reasons to agree	Reasons to disagree

Topic B: Companies should sell products any way they can.	
Reasons to agree	Reasons to disagree

Answer the questions. Then choose the topic for your paragraph.

▸ Which topic do you have a strong opinion about?_____

▸ Which opinion can you support with good reasons?_____

K OUTLINE Complete the outline.

Title: _____

Topic sentence (include topic and opinion): _____

Supporting idea 1:	Supporting idea 2:
Detail(s):	Detail(s):

Concluding sentence: _____

L FIRST DRAFT Use your outline to write a first draft of your paragraph.

M REVISE Use this list as you write your second draft.

☐ Does your topic sentence give your opinion?

☐ Do you give at least two supporting ideas/reasons for your opinion?

☐ Do you give details?

☐ Does the paragraph have a concluding sentence?

☐ Is there any information that doesn't belong?

N EDIT Use this list as you write your final draft.

☐ Do you use modals correctly?

☐ Do your subjects and verbs agree?

☐ Do you spell all the words correctly?

☐ Do you use correct capitalization and punctuation?

O FINAL DRAFT Reread your final draft and correct any errors. Then submit it to your teacher.

REFLECT

A Check (✓) the Reflect activities you can do and the academic skills you can use.

☐ think about your food buying habits

☐ understand how food labels affect you

☐ think critically about food choices

☐ analyze food labels

☐ write a paragraph about food

☐ identify facts and opinions

☐ write concluding sentences

☐ modals for suggestions and advice

☐ evaluate writers' claims

B Check (✓) the vocabulary words from the unit that you know. Circle words you still need to practice. Add any other words that you learned.

NOUN	VERB	ADJECTIVE	ADVERB & OTHER
customer	attract	natural	carefully
diet	convince	negative	instead
fast food	encourage	whole	
label	give up		
menu	include		
option	order		
product	select		
section			

C Reflect on the ideas in the unit as you answer these questions.

1. What else do you want to know about how companies sell food?

_____

_____

2. What ideas or skills in this unit will be most useful to you in the future?

_____

_____

6 | THE WONDERS OF NATURE

Tourists in a "water forest" at a park in Yangzhou in China's Jiangsu province

IN THIS UNIT

▸ Discuss your experiences in nature

▸ Rank the benefits of nature

▸ Identify sites to visit

▸ Investigate World Heritage Sites

▸ Describe a graph or chart about nature

SKILLS

READING
Understand the author's purpose

WRITING
Describe data

GRAMMAR
Infinitives and gerunds

CRITICAL THINKING
Analyze graphs and charts

CONNECT TO THE TOPIC

1. What is unusual about the park in this photo?

2. How does nature make you feel?

WATCH
HA LONG BAY

A ACTIVATE Discuss the meaning of the words with a partner. Look up any you don't know. Do you have these in your area?

bay	island	mountain	river	tunnel
cave	lake	ocean	rock	valley

B Watch the video. Check (✓) the words in activity A that you hear. ▶ 6.1

C Watch again. Read the sentences. Write T for *True*, F for *False*, or NG for *Not Given*. ▶ 6.1

1. _____ There are 1,600 islands in Ha Long Bay.

2. _____ Ha Long Bay is in the Philippines.

3. _____ Many people live on the islands.

4. _____ The name *Ha Long* means "flying bird."

5. _____ Many children believe the stories about the dragon.

6. _____ There are two national parks next to Ha Long Bay.

7. _____ Visitors can go kayaking and caving there.

Ha Long Bay, Vietnam

PREPARE TO READ

A VOCABULARY Read the sentences. Match the definitions to the words in bold.

a. (n) illegal activity
b. (n phr) natural land, not in towns or cities
c. (n) a large area of trees in nature
d. (v) to stop something from happening
e. (v phr) to use time doing something

f. (n) the things you can see from a place
g. (v) to become or make less
h. (adv) not inside a building
i. (n) worry
j. (adv) maybe

1. _____ Last year, I lived in the city, but now I live in **the country**.

2. _____ That neighborhood is dangerous. There's a lot of **crime**.

3. _____ More people buy homes when prices **decrease**.

4. _____ Do you like to be **outdoors**? Or do you enjoy being inside?

5. _____ Colin is late. **Perhaps** he missed the bus.

6. _____ The city wanted to **prevent** car accidents. It added more traffic lights.

7. _____ Teenagers **spend** a lot of **time** with their friends.

8. _____ I'm feeling a lot of **stress**. I have problems at work.

9. _____ There's a **view** of downtown London from the roof of this building.

10. _____ I like to walk in the **woods** near my house. The trees are very tall there.

B PERSONALIZE Answer the questions.

1. How much **time** do you **spend outdoors**? _____

2. What are some good ways to **decrease stress**, in your experience?

_____

3. Where do you want to live—in the city or **the country**? Explain.

_____

REFLECT   Discuss your experiences in nature.

You are going to read about the benefits of being in nature. Work with a partner and discuss the questions.

1. Do you like to be outside in nature?

2. Where do you like to go?

3. What activities do you like to do outside?

READ

READING TIP

When you **skim** a text, you read quickly to get the general idea. This helps you predict the information in the text. As you skim, don't read every word. Instead, look for important or repeated words and phrases. Also, read the first and last paragraphs and the first sentence of the other paragraphs.

A PREDICT Skim the article. Check (✓) the sentences you think are true.

1. _____ Being outdoors in nature has many benefits.

2. _____ Nature improves our health.

3. _____ Nature doesn't change the way we feel.

4. _____ Green spaces in cities make crime go up.

5. _____ One disadvantage of spending time in nature is the cost.

B Read the article. Check your answers in activity A.

C MAIN IDEAS The article has six paragraphs. Match the paragraph number to each description.

a. _____ It explains the economic benefits of nature.

b. _____ It introduces the importance of nature.

c. _____ It summarizes why nature is important.

d. _____ It describes the effects of nature on mental health.

e. _____ It explains the benefits for the community.

f. _____ It explains how physical health improves.

A woman takes a walk in the woods in Italy.

A WALK IN THE WOODS 🎧6.1

1   "I took a walk in the **woods** and came out taller than the trees," said Henry David Thoreau. Thoreau was an American writer in the 1900s. He believed in the positive effects of nature. Today we know there are many benefits of nature in our lives.

2   Thoreau felt stronger after a walk in **the country**. Recent research agrees. Researchers from the U.K. looked at 140 studies from around the world. When people **spend time** in nature, they have fewer diseases, such as heart disease. Research in Japan shows walking in the woods may also **prevent** cancer. In addition, children who live near parks are more fit and see better. Hospital patients with **views** of trees get better more quickly. Nature is good for our physical health.

3   **Perhaps** even more important are the mental[1] health benefits. Nature helps us feel more positive. When people did something in nature for 30 days, they reported greater happiness. Children had better concentration[2]. And adults felt less **stress**. You don't need to go outside every day. People get the benefits with only two hours **outdoors** each week. Even playing video games with a view of nature helps.

4   When people feel happier and less stressed, it has positive effects on the whole community. Time in nature helps people feel closer to their community. This makes **crime decrease**. In general, more green space leads to fewer violent[3] crimes. The community is healthier overall.

5   Another benefit of nature is economic[4]. Happier, healthier people have a better quality of life[5]. They need less medicine and fewer hospitals. People miss less work, so businesses do better. Researchers say better quality of life is worth $6 trillion a year around the world. Nature is good for the economy.

6   In today's world, we don't always have time to go outdoors. We can become too busy with school, work, and relationships. But our relationship with nature is very important. Time in nature has many benefits. And they are available to everyone for free. A walk in the woods might make us all feel taller than the trees.

---

[1]**mental** (adj) relating to the mind or thinking

[2]**concentration** (n) the action of focusing attention on something

[3]**violent** (adj) using actions that hurt or kill someone

[4]**economic** (adj) relating to business or money

[5]**quality of life** (n phr) the health, comfort, and happiness experienced by a person or group

READING SKILL Understand the author's purpose

As you read, think about the author's **purpose**, or reason for writing the text. This will help you understand the text better. Authors write to inform, explain, persuade, or entertain. To identify the purpose, ask yourself if the author wants:

▸ to give you information? (to inform)
▸ to give reasons for or describe something? (to explain)
▸ you to act or think in a certain way? (to persuade)
▸ to give you something interesting or funny to read? (to entertain)

D APPLY Read the article again. Choose the author's purpose.

    a. to entertain   b. to persuade   c. to inform

E DETAILS Answer the questions. Write one to three words or numbers from the article.

1. The article begins with a quote. Who said it? _____

2. How many studies did researchers in the U.K. look at? _____

3. Who improves with a view of trees? _____

4. How much time do you need to spend outdoors each week to feel less stress?

    _____

5. What leads to fewer violent crimes? _____

6. How much is a better quality of life worth a year? _____

REFLECT Rank the benefits of nature.

Look at the list of benefits from the article. Rank them (1 = most important, 10 = least important). Compare ideas with a partner.

_____ more able to concentrate   _____ greater fitness

_____ a closer community   _____ less missed work

_____ less violent crime   _____ better quality of life

_____ fewer diseases   _____ less stress

_____ getting better more quickly   _____ more positive feelings

PREPARE TO READ

A VOCABULARY Complete the sentences with the correct words.

at least (phr)	history (n)	protect (v)	replace (v)	tourist (n)
damage (v)	list (n)	region (n)	site (n)	wonderful (adj)

1. That movie was _____. I want to see it again.

2. There are _____ 20 different kinds of animals in the park near my house.

3. Bad storms often _____ houses and other buildings.

4. Conservationists want to _____ animals and plants in danger.

5. Pam loves to visit Italy. Her favorite _____ is in the north, but she likes all areas.

6. Istanbul is an important city in world _____. Many things happened there.

7. Rhinos are on a(n) _____ of animals in danger.

8. The _____ asked for information about the Louvre and the Eiffel Tower.

9. The Colosseum is a famous _____ in Rome.

10. A new office building will _____ the old shopping mall.

B Complete the paragraph with the correct form of the words from activity A.

Paris

There are many great places in Europe, but Paris is one of the most ¹_____ cities

in that ²_____. It attracts ³_____ 30 million ⁴_____ each year.

People come to see its many beautiful buildings and monuments. However, new businesses are

moving in. New buildings are ⁵_____ older buildings. In 2024, two new towers will be

on a large ⁶_____ which is now full of apartments. Residents weren't able to

⁷_____ their homes, but there will be more jobs. Like other cities, Paris has to change in

some ways to grow.

REFLECT Identify sites to visit.

You are going to read about important sites around the world. Work with a partner and discuss the questions.

1. What are some important sites in your country or region? Why are they important?

2. What activities do people do in those sites?

WORLD HERITAGE SITES

A PREDICT *Heritage* means "places, art, customs, and beliefs that are important to a culture." What do you think World Heritage Sites are? Do you know any of them? Read the travel blog and check your answers.

B MAIN IDEAS Check (✓) the four main ideas.

1. _____ UNESCO wants to protect sites of cultural, historical, and scientific importance.

2. _____ Some sites protect culture, others protect nature, and some do both.

3. _____ World Heritage Sites include some of the Seven Wonders of the World.

4. _____ There are well-known sites, as well as new sites.

5. _____ The most natural sites are in Asia and the Pacific.

6. _____ UNESCO identifies sites in danger.

An ice cave in Vatnajökull National Park, Iceland

1   The Seven Wonders of the World are famous, but many people don't know about UNESCO[1] World Heritage Sites. There are more than 1,100 UNESCO **sites** in 167 countries. Do you want to see some of the most **wonderful** locations in the world? Then put these on your **list**.

2   **Q: What is a World Heritage Site?**

A: World Heritage Sites are important for their culture, science, or **history**. The United Nations wants to **protect** them. There are three types: cultural, natural, and mixed. Some places have important buildings, art, or customs. Others tell us about our planet or about unusual plants and animals. Some sites are a single building. Others include many buildings, or even whole cities! When a site is put on the UNESCO list, people want to protect it.

3   **Q: What are some examples of World Heritage Sites?**

A: Famous examples include Machu Picchu, the city of Kyoto, and the Pyramids at Giza. Bagan is an old city in Myanmar. It is a new cultural site on the list. It has beautiful art and buildings. They are about 1,000 years old. The Vatnajökull National Park in Iceland is a new natural site. It has 10 volcanoes[2] and covers **at least** 1.4

million hectares. There is a new mixed site in Brazil. It includes the historic town of Paraty and nearby natural areas. Some animals there, such as jaguars[3], are in danger.

4   **Q: Where are the most World Heritage Sites?**

A: Europe and North America have the most cultural sites (453). They have about half of all of the cultural sites on the list. The most natural sites are in Asia and the Pacific. The fewest sites are in the Arab states.

5   **Q: What does it mean if a Heritage Site is in danger?**

A: UNESCO identifies sites in danger. These dangers include disasters, development, and tourism. For example, hurricanes **damage** the Everglades. New buildings are **replacing** historic ones in Zabid, Yemen. And Vienna and Venice are in danger because of too many **tourists**! It's important to save these wonderful places. After all, UNESCO made the list for this exact reason.

[1] **UNESCO** (n) United Nations Educational, Scientific and Cultural Organization

[2] **volcano** (n) a mountain that sometimes pushes out hot liquid rock and gas through a hole at the top

[3] **jaguar** (n) a large, wild cat that lives in Latin America

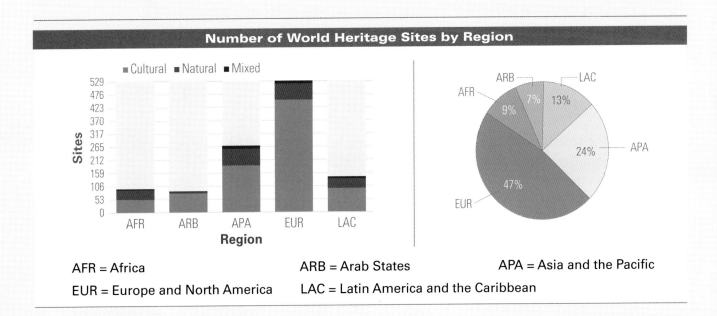

Number of World Heritage Sites by Region

AFR = Africa   ARB = Arab States   APA = Asia and the Pacific

EUR = Europe and North America   LAC = Latin America and the Caribbean

C DETAILS Read the sentences. Use information from the travel blog and the graphics. Write T for *True* or F for *False*.

1. _____ There are World Heritage Sites in 200 countries.

2. _____ A World Heritage Site can be only one building.

3. _____ A new natural site is in Bagan, Myanmar.

4. _____ Paraty, Brazil, is an example of a mixed site.

5. _____ Vienna is in danger because of development.

6. _____ Europe and North America have more natural sites than cultural sites.

7. _____ There are about 100 total sites in Africa.

8. _____ The Arab states have more cultural sites than natural sites.

9. _____ The author's purpose is to entertain the reader.

D Discuss the questions with a partner.

1. Which of the three types of sites do you think is most important? Why?

2. Which of the sites in the travel blog do you want to visit? Why?

3. Should tourists visit sites in danger? Explain.

REFLECT   Investigate World Heritage Sites.

Work with a small group. Assign one of the sites from the travel blog to each person. Go online or to the library to find information about the site. Why is it on the list? Write notes in your notebook. Share your research with your group. As a group, rank the sites in order of which ones you want to visit most.

WRITE

UNIT TASK Describe a graph or chart about nature.

> You are going to write a paragraph to describe data from a graph or chart. This is a common academic task, and it is sometimes on tests. Use the ideas, vocabulary, and skills from the unit.

A MODEL Read the paragraph. Underline the topic sentence.

Favorite Park Activities

The bar graph shows why Americans went to parks in 2018. Overall, people went to the park to relax more than to play sports or race. Fifty-eight percent went to the park to get together with family and friends. About half (48 percent) relaxed at the pool. Many visited a park to walk or hike on trails. About a third went to community events. Only about 1 in 10 played team sports or ran in races in the park. In conclusion, more Americans went to the park to be with people and relax than to compete.

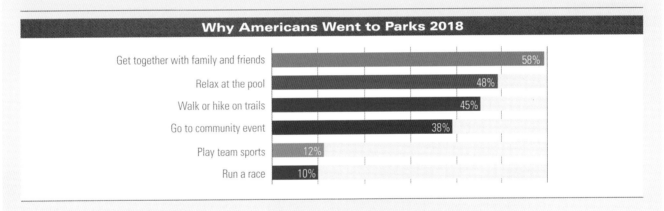

Why Americans Went to Parks 2018

Get together with family and friends	58%
Relax at the pool	48%
Walk or hike on trails	45%
Go to community event	38%
Play team sports	12%
Run a race	10%

WRITING SKILL Describe data

You find **data**, or information about numbers, in:
- bar and line graphs
- pie charts
- tables or charts with columns and rows

When you describe data, follow these steps:

1. Introduce the subject. *The graph/chart/table shows* + information from the title of the graphic.

2. Describe the most important point(s) or the overall trend. A trend is a general development or change. Point out highest or lowest numbers, or biggest changes.

3. Give a few interesting details with numbers. It is not important to describe every detail. Focus on the main point(s).

B APPLY Reread the model paragraph. Double underline the most important point. Circle the numerical information.

C ANALYZE THE MODEL Complete the outline of the model paragraph.

1. **Introduction sentence:** _____

2. **Most important point:** _____

   Detail 1: _____

   Detail 2: _____

   Detail 3: _____

   Detail 4: _____

   Detail 5: _____

3. **Concluding sentence:** _____

WRITING TIP

You can describe numbers or percentages in different ways.

100%	all	50%	half
90%	almost all	35%	about a third
75%	most, three-quarters	25%	a quarter, one-fourth
60%	more than half	10%	1 in 10, a small number

People enjoy the park along the Han River in Seoul, South Korea.

D Choose the correct descriptions of the percentages to complete the paragraph.

Why South Koreans Visit Parks

The table shows the reasons people visit national parks in South Korea. One reason is much more common than the others. ¹**More than half / Less than half / Three-quarters** (58%) go to parks to become healthier. ²**A quarter / One-fifth / Most** (20%) go to relax. ³**Many / A quarter / About 1 in 10** (13%) want to build friendship. Only ⁴**about one in five / a small number / about a third** (8%) want to experience the outdoors. The main reason South Koreans visit their parks is to be healthier.

Reason for visiting South Korean national parks	Percentage
To become healthier	58%
To relax	20%
To build friendship	13%
To experience nature/outdoors	8%
Other	1%

GRAMMAR Infinitives and gerunds

We use **infinitives** (*to* + base form of verb) after certain verbs, such as *want, need,* and *plan.*

   *Many visitors **want to take** a tour.*

We use **infinitives of purpose** to give a reason or to answer the question *Why?*

   *Not many people **go** to the park **to hike**.*

We use **gerunds** (verb + *-ing*) as the subject of a sentence or as the object of certain verbs, such as *discuss, enjoy,* and *finish.* We often use gerunds for activities. Gerund subjects are always singular.

For most verbs, add *-ing.*	*Many people enjoy **walking**.*
For verbs ending in *-e,* drop the *-e* and add *-ing.*	***Hiking** is a popular activity.*
For one-syllable verbs ending in vowel-consonant, double the consonant and add *-ing.*	***Planning** trips is a lot of fun.*

E GRAMMAR Complete the paragraph with the infinitive or gerund form of the verbs.

Visitors to Costa Rica

The bar graph shows the top activities of visitors to Costa Rica. Overall, most tourists go to Costa Rica ¹_____ (do) outdoor activities. More than half (57%) want ²_____ (go) to the beach or sit in the sun. ³_____ (hike) is a reason for almost half (45.5%) of the visitors. About the same number go to Costa Rica ⁴_____ (visit) the volcanoes. About 40% want ⁵_____ (see) plants and animals. ⁶_____ (shop) was a top activity for only about a third of the visitors. It's clear that outdoor activities attract the most visitors to this wonderful country.

F GRAMMAR Answer the questions. Use infinitives or gerunds.

1. Why do you go to parks or other green spaces?

   _____

2. Do you need to get out in nature sometimes? Explain.

   _____

3. What are your favorite outdoor activities?

   _____

G EDIT Read the paragraph. Find and correct five errors with gerunds or infinitives.

Visiting Parks in Canada

The table shows the results of research about Parks Canada visitors in 2017. Visitors enjoyed to be outdoors most of all. Experience nature was the main attraction for about half the visitors (52%). For some (16%), climbing and to hike were the most enjoyable parts. About the same number of people visited the park because of the lakes, rivers, or other places with water. Seeing animals were important to a smaller number of visitors (7%). This graph shows most visitors want to go to parks experiencing nature.

PLAN & WRITE

H PLAN Look at the bar graph and pie chart. What is the most important point of each one? Write it down. Then choose one to write about.

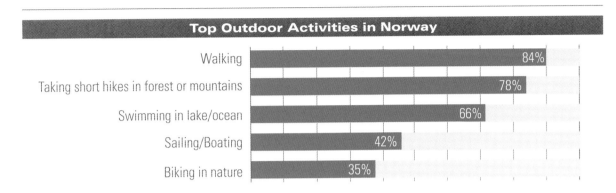

Most important point: _____

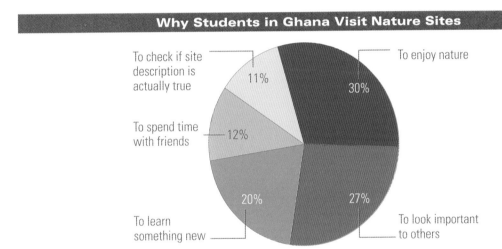

Most important point: _____

I OUTLINE Complete the outline for your paragraph.

1. **Introduction sentence:** _____

2. **Most important point:** _____

   Detail 1: _____

   Detail 2: _____

   Detail 3: _____

   Detail 4: _____

3. **Concluding sentence:** _____

J FIRST DRAFT Use your outline to write a first draft of your paragraph.

K REVISE Use this list as you write your second draft.

- ☐ Do you introduce the graph/chart?
- ☐ Do you give the most important point or overall trend?
- ☐ Do you use a variety of words to describe the data?
- ☐ Does the paragraph have a concluding sentence?
- ☐ Is there any information that doesn't belong?

L EDIT Use this list as you write your final draft.

- ☐ Do you use infinitives and gerunds correctly?
- ☐ Do your subjects and verbs agree?
- ☐ Do you spell all the words correctly?
- ☐ Do you use correct capitalization and punctuation?

M FINAL DRAFT Reread your final draft and correct any errors. Then submit it to your teacher.

The aurora borealis (also called the polar or northern lights) at Grosbeak Lake, Wood Buffalo National Park, Alberta, Canada

REFLECT

A Check (✓) the Reflect activities you can do and the academic skills you can use.

☐ discuss your experiences in nature

☐ rank the benefits of nature

☐ identify sites to visit

☐ investigate World Heritage Sites

☐ describe a graph or chart about nature

☐ understand the author's purpose

☐ describe data

☐ infinitives and gerunds

☐ analyze graphs and charts

B Check (✓) the vocabulary words from the unit that you know. Circle words you still need to practice. Add any other words that you learned.

NOUN	VERB	ADJECTIVE	ADVERB & OTHER
the country	damage	wonderful	at least
crime	decrease		outdoors
history	prevent		perhaps
list	protect		
region	replace		
site	spend time		
stress			
tourist			
view			
woods			

C Reflect on the ideas in the unit as you answer these questions.

1. In what ways could spending time in nature help you? Which benefit do you need the most right now?

_____

_____

2. What ideas or skills in this unit will be most useful to you in the future?

_____

_____

Competitors take part in The Red Bull Soapbox Race in London, England. They make their own racecars.

IN THIS UNIT

▶ Define success and failure

▶ Explore ideas about success and failure

▶ Consider how to be successful in an interview

▶ Compare responses

▶ Write a paragraph about learning from failure

SKILLS

READING
Annotate a text

WRITING
Write coherently

GRAMMAR
Present perfect

CRITICAL THINKING
Compare and contrast

CONNECT TO THE TOPIC

1. Do you think these drivers will win the race? Why or why not?

2. What do *success* and *failure* mean? Do you learn more when you fail or when you succeed?

111

National Geographic Explorer Gabby Salazar with colleague Clare Fiesler and Moreangels Mbizah in Zimbabwe

FACING CHALLENGES

A Match the words to the definitions. Use a dictionary if necessary.

1. balance
2. barrier
3. challenge
4. pursue

a. something that makes it hard to do something
b. to give equal attention to two or more things
c. a rule or problem that makes something difficult
d. to try to get or do something over time

B Look at the title and the photo. Answer the questions.

1. What do you think it means to face challenges?
2. What barriers do you think the people in the photo face?

C Watch the video. Write T for *True* or F for *False*. Correct the false statements. ▶ 7.1

1. _____ Gabby Salazar is a photographer and filmmaker.

2. _____ Moreangels Mbizah studies lions in Ghana.

3. _____ Gabby's advice is "Don't become a scientist."

PREPARE TO READ

A VOCABULARY Complete the sentences with the correct form of the words.

amount (n)	even (adv)	finally (adv)	pay attention (v phr)	prepare (v)
depend on (v phr)	feeling (n)	motivated (adj)	pleasant (adj)	recent (adj)

1. I went to the dentist today. It wasn't _____, but my teeth are clean and healthy.

2. We need to _____ for Rob's visit. He arrives tomorrow, and there is a lot to do.

3. I got an A on the test, and I didn't _____ study!

4. Mia waited for a long time for the bus. It _____ came at 9:30 a.m.

5. The _____ article about video games was interesting. It was in the last week or two.

6. It's hard for me to _____ in class today. I can't concentrate very well.

7. Jorge is an excellent student. He gets high grades. He is _____ to succeed.

8. My _____ about travel are mixed. I enjoy it, but it makes me feel stressed.

9. Our grade _____ three things: tests, homework, and class discussion.

10. There's a large _____ of information about failure in the article.

B PERSONALIZE Complete the sentences to make them true for you.

1. I am **motivated** when _____.

2. I always **prepare** for _____.

3. One **recent** challenge in my life was _____.

4. For me, success in school **depends on** _____.

REFLECT   Define success and failure.

You are going to read about success and failure. What do these words mean to you?
Work with a group. Give examples of success and failure in these three areas.

School	Work	Family
getting a good grade		

READ

FROM **FAILURE** TO **SUCCESS**

A PREVIEW Look at the title, photo, and caption. Then answer the questions.

1. What is the article about?

   a. How failure hurts people

   b. Famous people who failed and succeeded

   c. When failure has positive effects

2. How could this team fail? How could they succeed?

1   Failure often isn't **pleasant**, but does it help or hurt us? For media executive Oprah Winfrey, failure is a stepping stone to success. For international actress Lupita Nyong'o, failure helps her discover new things. For soccer player Lionel Messi, it's sometimes necessary in order to improve. Many famous people believe we learn from failure and need it to succeed. The positive effect of failure may **depend on** several factors[1].

2   First, **recent** research shows we learn best from a small **amount** of failure. How much? About 15 percent, according to a U.S. study. If a challenge is too easy, we don't learn anything. If it is too difficult, we stop trying. People, monkeys, and **even** computers learn the fastest when they get the answer right 85 percent of the time. Learning happens with the right amount of both failure and success.

3   Another factor is how we react, or what we do after a failure. In one study with college students, researchers made a task impossible, so everyone failed. Afterward, the students were put into two groups. Researchers encouraged one group of students to **pay attention** to their **feelings** about failure. The other group paid attention to their thoughts. Then everyone tried the task again. Those who paid attention to their feelings tried harder the second time. In a different study, some people took responsibility[2] for their mistakes, and some did not. The ones who took responsibility were more likely to succeed on a second task.

4   When you **prepare** for a task with a plan, it can also help. Researchers in Japan and Switzerland asked college students to write an essay. They gave half the students a plan for the essay. The others did not have one. Then the researchers stopped all students before they completed the task. Those with a plan were more **motivated** to finish. They wanted to try again.

5   Everyone experiences failure sometimes. Some people stop trying. Others try harder and **finally** succeed. The amount of failure, our reaction to it, and having a plan can make failure a positive experience. We need to take responsibility for mistakes and prepare for the next time. Then failure can be a path to success.

---

[1]**factor** (n) a fact or situation that changes or causes something else

[2]**take responsibility** (v phr) to say that you did something or caused something to happen

B MAIN IDEAS The article has five paragraphs. Match the paragraph numbers to each heading.

a. _____ How much failure?

b. _____ Different views of failure

c. _____ A path to success

d. _____ Reacting to failure

e. _____ Having a plan

The Icarus Cup is the world's most challenging human-powered-aircraft competition. This team hopes to complete the course before the rain starts.

C APPLY Annotate paragraphs 2–4 in the article. Then compare your annotations with a partner.

D DETAILS Complete the sentences with one word from the article.

1. Lionel Messi believes you need failure in order to _____.

2. People learn best when they have a(n) _____ amount of failure—about 15 percent.

3. People who pay attention to their _____ try harder next time.

4. We do better when we take _____ for mistakes.

5. Researchers from Japan and Switzerland asked students to write a(n) _____.

6. Students who had a(n) _____ wanted to finish their work.

E Discuss the questions with a partner.

1. How much challenge are you comfortable with? If a challenge is too difficult, do you stop trying?

2. How do you feel when you fail? Does paying attention to your feelings help or hurt you?

3. What makes you want to try harder after failure?

REFLECT Explore ideas about success and failure.

Go online and find two or three quotes about success or failure. Choose one that you agree with. Then write a few sentences about the quote. What does it mean? How does it relate to your experience? Then share your ideas with a small group.

PREPARE TO READ

A VOCABULARY Match the sentences on the left with the correct responses on the right.

1. ____ When did you know it was a problem?
2. ____ Did you **pick** Tyler **up** from the airport?
3. ____ I sent you an email. Did you get it?
4. ____ Do you really want to change schools?
5. ____ Can you **organize** the party?
6. ____ Are you going to help Nick move?
7. ____ Do you **judge** people you just met?
8. ____ How do you prepare for an **interview**?
9. ____ Are you working for the same **employer** as last year?
10. ____ I told the teacher I had to **miss** class.

a. Were you sick? Is that why you didn't go?
b. No, I didn't **receive** it.
c. Sure. I'm good at planning activities.
d. Yes, the way they dress and act helps me form an opinion of them.
e. No, he took a taxi.
f. I **realized** it last night.
g. He said no to my **offer**. He can do it alone.
h. Yes, I'm very **serious** about leaving.
i. I practice answering common questions.
j. No, I have a new job now.

REFLECT Consider how to be successful in an interview.

You are going to read about how to answer interview questions. What do you think makes a successful job interview? Look at the chart and answer the questions.

1. What four factors does this pie chart show?

   _____
   _____
   _____
   _____

2. What is the most important factor?

   _____
   _____

3. What other factors might be important in a job interview?

   _____
   _____

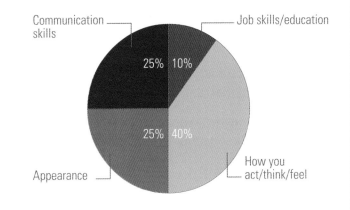

How Do People Judge You During a Job or College Interview?

Communication skills — 25%
Job skills/education — 10%
How you act/think/feel — 40%
Appearance — 25%

READ

A PREVIEW Read the title and the first paragraph. Then answer the questions.

1. How many writers are there? Why are they writing?
2. What do you want to ask a career coach?

READING TIP

Writers often have a **tone**. This is how they feel about the topic. Pay attention to words that show how they feel. For example, a writer's tone can be serious, funny, excited, angry, or confident.

B Read the advice column. Which words show that the writer feels bad or frustrated:

1. in paragraph 2?

   _____

   _____

2. in paragraph 3?

   _____

   _____

C MAIN IDEAS Put the main ideas in the order they are in the reading.

a. _____ The question "What is your greatest failure?" tells interviewers important things about a person.

b. _____ A good response shows you can change your approach.

c. _____ A good response shows you developed skills.

d. _____ The person with the question has trouble describing her "greatest failure."

e. _____ The career coach also thinks the question is difficult to answer.

Zhongshuge bookstore in Beijing, China

DESCRIBE YOUR GREATEST FAILURE 🎧 7.2

1   It isn't easy to choose a career. And when you have a career, it can be hard to know how to develop in that job. Career coaches help people get new jobs, or grow in the ones they have. Coaches sometimes write advice columns where they answer letters from readers. Here is a career advice column, with a question to (Q) and an answer from (A) a career coach.

2   **Q:** I need your advice. I've had several job **interviews**, but I haven't **received** a job **offer** yet. I feel terrible. I need help answering interview questions. One question that I find difficult is "What is your greatest failure?" In one interview, I described a big failure at work. I sent the project to the wrong person, and the company lost both customers. Later, I **realized** this story made me look really bad. In the next interview, I said I got a low grade on an exam in college. That time, the interviewer looked bored with my answer. What am I doing wrong?

3   **A:** I <u>really</u> don't like this question, but many **employers** ask it. Your experiences show the problem with it. If you describe a terrible failure in the same type of job, the employer might think you'll fail in this job, too. If you talk about something small, like a bad grade long ago, the interviewer may think you aren't **serious** enough.

4   Why do interviewers ask this question? It tells them about you. Are you confident enough to talk about your past failures? Are you able to **judge** your own performance[1] and see where you can improve? Do you learn and grow from challenging situations?

5   Here's my advice. Describe a failure that you have learned from. Here are two example responses to the interview question "What is your greatest failure?":

6   **Recent college graduate:** *I needed a job in college. The bookstore needed someone to **organize** events. I love books, and I like talking to customers. However, I didn't know a lot about preparing for events. One day, I forgot to **pick up** an author from the airport. He **missed** the reading at the bookstore. Since then, I've worked hard on my organizational skills. Now I am the event planner at a hotel.*

7   **Soccer coach:** *I have played and coached adult soccer for many years. A few years ago, I started to coach kids. I coached them the same way I coached adults. I was too hard on them. They didn't enjoy playing. One of the other coaches talked to me. I thought about what helped me as a kid, and I changed my approach[2]. I've tried to use that experience in all my jobs since then. I'm ready to change if something doesn't work.*

---

[1] **performance** (n) how well or badly you do something

[2] **approach** (n) a way of thinking about or doing something

D DETAILS Read the sentences. Write T for *True,* F for *False,* or NG for *Not Given.*

1. _____ The person with the question had a job at a marketing company.

2. _____ The person with the question wants a job offer.

3. _____ The person with the question thinks her answers aren't good yet.

4. _____ The career coach thinks all interview questions are good.

5. _____ Describing a failure can show you are confident.

6. _____ The career coach thinks the person should not describe a real failure.

7. _____ In the recent college graduate example, the employee was not good at organizing.

8. _____ The recent college graduate took classes to improve.

9. _____ The soccer coach worked with kids for many years.

10. _____ The kids didn't enjoy playing soccer when the coach started.

CRITICAL THINKING   Compare and contrast

When you **compare** two things, you pay attention to similarities, or the ways they are alike. When you **contrast** two things, you notice their differences. Comparing and contrasting helps you analyze and evaluate things.

REFLECT   Compare responses.

Copy the Venn diagram in your notebook and use it to compare and contrast the two examples in the career advice column. Take notes on the recent college graduate in the left section, the soccer coach in the right section, and the things both have in common in the middle. What makes a good interview response?

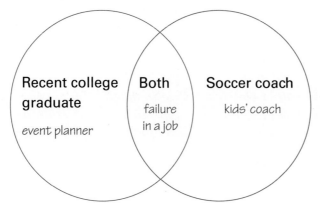

WRITE

UNIT TASK Write a paragraph about learning from failure.

Imagine you are responding to a common question in a job interview or college application: "Describe a failure and explain what you learned from it." Use the ideas, vocabulary, and skills from the unit.

A MODEL Read the paragraph. Underline the topic sentence.

Learning the Hard Way

One of my early failures taught me an important lesson about asking for help. In my science class, everyone had to give an important presentation. Most of the final grade for the class depended on the presentation. For the assignment, the teacher told us to include graphic information. There were a few things I didn't understand about the assignment. Unfortunately, as I prepared, I didn't ask any questions. I also didn't ask for help. In the end, I didn't include the right kind of data, or use graphs. The presentation was terrible. I almost failed the class. Since then, I have changed the way I prepare. Now, I ask questions when I don't understand something, and I also ask for help when I need it. It was a hard lesson to learn, but now I am a better student.

B ANALYZE THE MODEL Annotate the model paragraph. Mark the following information in the text.

1. Background information (2 sentences)
2. Story of the failure (7 sentences)
3. Lesson learned (2 sentences)
4. Concluding sentence

WRITING SKILL Write coherently

Writing is **coherent** when all of the ideas are well organized and well connected. When a paragraph is coherent, the ideas are clear and easy to understand. Coherent writing:

▶ uses logical order

I coached them the same way I coached adults. I was too hard on them. They didn't enjoy playing. (The first sentence is a statement of fact. The next two sentences explain why it was a problem.)

▶ repeats key words

*I have played and **coached adult** soccer for many years. A few years ago, I started to **coach** kids. I **coached** them the same way I **coached adults**.*

▶ uses transition words and phrases

***However**, I didn't know a lot about preparing for events. **One day**, I forgot to pick up an author from the airport. He missed the reading at the bookstore. **Since then**, I've worked hard on my organizational skills.*

WRITING TIP

Use **transition words and phrases** to make your ideas easier to understand.

▶ Giving time order: *first, second, then, next, later, since then*

▶ Giving examples: *for example, for instance*

▶ Adding different information: *however*

▶ Adding similar information: *also, in addition*

C APPLY Choose the correct transition words or phrases to complete the paragraph. Then underline repeated words.

Try, Try Again

One of my greatest childhood successes started out as a failure. I joined the track team in school. I liked running. ¹**Also / However**, I wanted more exercise. I wasn't tall like most short-distance runners, so the coach put me in longer races. ²**Finally / However**, I wanted to run in the shorter, faster races. I thought the 100-meter race was very exciting. My coach finally put me in a 100m event. I came in last. It was a terrible performance. What did I do? I began to run every day, both short and long distances. ³**In addition / For example**, I exercised to improve my strength. ⁴**For instance / Since then**, I jumped onto a high box every day. I became much stronger. I also became much faster. ⁵**However / Finally**, after weeks of work, my coach put me in another short race, and I won! I learned something important. If you want something very much and you work very hard, you can achieve your goals.

F GRAMMAR Answer the questions.

1. What is one important success you have had?

   _____

2. How have you changed because of that success?

   _____

3. What is one mistake you have made as a student?

   _____

G EDIT Read the paragraph. Find and correct five errors with the present perfect.

The Hardest Challenge

One of the hardest challenges I have face is moving to another country. I have always be close to my family and friends. My parents have helped me in many ways. They've encourage me. My friends have always been there for me also. Living far away from them was very difficult, and I felt very alone. Since my move, I try to stay in contact with family and friends as much as possible. We communicate by text and video chat. It not has been easy, but I've grown stronger because of this challenge.

PLAN & WRITE

H BRAINSTORM What are three examples of a failure or mistake you have made? What have you learned from those experiences? Take notes.

Failure/Mistake	What I have learned

Review your notes. Which example is the strongest? Use that example as the topic for your paragraph.

I OUTLINE Complete the outline.

1. **Title:** _____

2. **Topic sentence:** _____

3. **Background information (2–3 sentences):**

_____

_____

4. **Story of the failure (4–7 sentences):**

_____

_____

_____

_____

5. **Lesson(s) learned (1–2 sentences):**

_____

6. **Concluding sentence:** _____

J FIRST DRAFT Use your outline to write a first draft of your paragraph.

K REVISE Use this list as you write your second draft.
- ☐ Do you have a topic sentence?
- ☐ Do you give necessary background information?
- ☐ Do you tell information in a logical order?
- ☐ Do you use transition words and repetition?
- ☐ Does the paragraph have a concluding sentence?
- ☐ Is there any information that doesn't belong?

L EDIT Use this list as you write your final draft.
- ☐ Do you use the present perfect correctly?
- ☐ Do your subjects and verbs agree?
- ☐ Do you spell all the words correctly?
- ☐ Do you use correct capitalization and punctuation?

M FINAL DRAFT Reread your final draft and correct any errors. Then submit it to your teacher.

REFLECT

A Check (✓) the Reflect activities you can do and the academic skills you can use.

☐ define success and failure

☐ annotate a text

☐ explore ideas about success and failure

☐ write coherently

☐ consider how to be successful in an interview

☐ present perfect

☐ compare responses

☐ compare and contrast

☐ write a paragraph about learning from failure

B Check (✓) the vocabulary words from the unit that you know. Circle words you still need to practice. Add any other words that you learned.

NOUN	VERB	ADJECTIVE	ADVERB & OTHER
amount	depend on	motivated	even
employer	judge	pleasant	finally
feeling	miss	recent	
interview	organize	serious	
offer	pay attention		
	pick up		
	prepare		
	realize		
	receive		

C Reflect on the ideas in the unit as you answer these questions.

1. In what ways can you use your failures to improve?

_____

_____

2. What ideas or skills in this unit will be most useful to you in the future?

_____

_____

UNIT
8 | SENDING THE RIGHT MESSAGE

IN THIS UNIT

▸ Analyze communication across generations

▸ Communicate tone in a message

▸ Brainstorm tips for texting

▸ Choose appropriate communication

▸ Write a formal email

SKILLS

READING
Understand pronoun reference

WRITING
Write an email to a teacher

GRAMMAR
Review of the present continuous

Review of the future

CRITICAL THINKING
Determine appropriate communication

This art project shows thousands of personal video diaries posted online. It is part of the Big Bang Data exhibit at the Centre de Cultura Contemporània de Barcelona, Spain.

CONNECT TO THE TOPIC

1. Why do people make video diaries?

2. How has the Internet changed the way people communicate?

People on their phones at a mall in Beijing, China

PHONE FOCUS

A PREVIEW Look at the photo. Answer the questions.

1. Does this scene look normal? _____

_____

2. Do you think people use their cell phones more for texting or for calling?

_____

3. When people use their phones, can they do other things at the same time?

_____

B Watch the video. Read the sentences. Write T for *True* or F for *False*. ▶8.1

1. _____ The invitation is to watch a game on television.

2. _____ The person inviting them will have pizza.

3. _____ Everyone invited will go.

4. _____ Other people offer to bring food, too.

5. _____ Someone will bring chocolate dessert.

C Watch again. What is happening in the background? Take notes. Then compare your notes with a partner. ▶8.1

D Watch part of the video again. Do the text messages use correct capitalization, punctuation, and grammar? Take notes on examples. Then discuss with a small group. ▶8.2

PREPARE TO READ

A VOCABULARY Complete the sentences with the correct form of the words.

comment (n)	generation (n)	probably (adv)	required (adj)	sort (n)
generally (adv)	informal (adj)	purpose (n)	shout (v)	technology (n)

1. I always buy the same _____ of running shoes. I've tried other kinds but I don't like them.

2. We use technology for many different _____.

3. Young people often have different opinions than people in their parents' _____.

4. Andrew is _____ at home because his car is parked in front.

5. You don't need to _____. I can hear you.

6. Some people have difficulty learning to use new _____, including phones.

7. I usually take the subway to work. It is _____ faster than driving. It's almost never slower.

8. The party will be very _____. You can wear casual clothes.

9. His _____ on my paper were helpful. Now I will revise it.

10. English 101 is a(n) _____ class. All first-year students have to take it.

REFLECT Analyze communication across generations.

You are going to read about how people communicate using the Internet. Think about your experiences. Then work with a partner to complete the chart.

Communication style	Your generation	Older generations
Technology used		
Formal or informal		
Use of punctuation		

WRITING ON THE INTERNET

Teenagers like these girls in Los Angeles, CA, USA, are ready to try new things and explore new ways to communicate and express themselves.

A PREDICT Skim the article. Then read the messages on the right. What is each person saying? How do these writers communicate their feelings?

hey
how's it going

But whyyyyy

WHAT HAVE YOU DONE

Sounds good!!!!

1   How is the Internet changing the way we write? Gretchen McCulloch answers this question in her 2019 book, *Because Internet*. McCulloch is a Canadian language researcher. She studies **informal** writing online. She looks at social media posts and blog **comments**. Some people think the Internet is making writing worse. McCulloch disagrees. She thinks changes from one **generation** to the next show the language is healthy. She has found some interesting patterns on changes in writing.

2   **The Internet is changing writing in many ways.** There are new words such as *vlog* and abbreviations such as *lol*. The use of correct grammar is no longer always **required**. Perhaps the most interesting changes are in the use of letters, spaces, punctuation, and emoji. Writers use them instead of tone of voice[1] or gestures[2]. Writers can **shout** or show strong feeling with ALL CAPS. Repeating letters or using spaces (y e s s s s) can also show feelings such as friendliness or excitement. Punctuation shows tone, too. Exclamation points (!) are more common now, especially more than one. Also, informal writers don't always end sentences with periods. Many writers use emoji such as ☺, 👍, or 👏 instead of gestures to communicate their ideas.

3   **Teenagers (14–18) are leading the changes,** especially girls, and young people in cities. They have bigger and closer communities. And they are ready to try new things. Young people are setting new trends[3] in writing, just like they do in fashion and music. They are exploring all **sorts** of new ways to communicate.

4   **Change is happening quickly because of both close and casual relationships.** If one of your close friends uses a new word, you are more likely to pick it up[4]. However, close friends **probably** share the same vocabulary. New ideas, including new words, **generally** come from outside close relationships—from casual or online friends. The Internet connects us to many more people, so language changes spread faster online. Think about how quickly a funny video becomes popular with millions of people.

5   McCulloch sees more change in the future. People will communicate online for many **purposes**. They will meet for work, take classes, and connect with people even more. New **technology** will help people communicate even better. And as they do, their language will certainly change and grow.

---

[1]**tone of voice** (n phr) the way a person speaks (volume, speed, etc.)

[2]**gesture** (n) a movement with your hand or body, such as smiling, pointing, or clapping

[3]**set a trend** (v phr) to start doing something that other people copy

[4]**pick up** (v phr) to learn

B MAIN IDEAS Read the sentences. Write T for *True*, F for *False*, or NG for *Not Given*.

1. _____ Gretchen McCulloch studies informal writing on the Internet.

2. _____ She only studies changes in the English language.

3. _____ The way things look on the page (use of letters, spaces, etc.) shows tone of voice.

4. _____ People in their 20s are most important in changing writing.

5. _____ Our use of new language comes from close friends, not casual friends.

6. _____ Healthy languages continue to change.

READING SKILL Understand pronoun reference

As you read, pay attention to **pronouns**. Writers use pronouns instead of nouns so they don't have to repeat the same words. Pronouns take the place of nouns and noun phrases. To check your understanding, say the sentence and replace the pronoun with the noun or noun phrase.

__McCulloch__ is a Canadian language researcher. __She__ studies informal writing online.

If one of your close friends uses __a new word__, you are more likely to pick __it__ up.

C APPLY Find the underlined pronouns in the reading. Complete the sentences.

1. The pronoun *them* in paragraph 2 refers to _____.

2. The pronoun *They* in paragraph 3 refers to _____.

3. The pronoun *it* in paragraph 4 refers to _____.

4. The pronoun *They* in paragraph 5 refers to _____.

D DETAILS Match the two sentence parts.

1. _____ The title of McCulloch's book is
2. _____ Social media posts and blog comments are examples of
3. _____ Writers use emoji
4. _____ You can use ALL CAPS, or capital letters,
5. _____ Girls are more likely than boys
6. _____ The Internet introduces us to

a. more casual friends.
b. instead of gestures.
c. to shout.
d. *Because Internet.*
e. informal online writing.
f. to lead language change.

REFLECT   Communicate tone in a message.

Write a message. Then use spaces, letters (capital/small, repeating, etc.), and punctuation to communicate three different meanings for the same message. Exchange messages with a partner and discuss possible meanings.

PREPARE TO READ

A VOCABULARY Complete the sentences with the correct form of the words. Then answer the questions with a partner.

---
choice (n)   enough (adj)   interrupt (v)   reply (v)   suggestion (n)

distance (n)   immediately (adv) polite (adj)   still (adv)   text message (n phr)
---

1. You are writing your teacher an email. Which is a more
   _____ way to end—*Regards* or *Bye*?

2. About how many _____ do you receive every day? Do
   you think that is normal?

3. What is the best way to travel a long _____?

4. Do you answer texts _____, or do you wait? Explain.

5. Do you usually _____ to emails the same day you
   receive them? Explain.

6. What is one _____ you can give to a new student about
   learning English?

7. Should students ever _____ their teachers? Or should
   they let them finish talking?

8. Do you have _____ information about writing emails in
   English? If not, what do you need to know?

9. Do you think a text message or a phone call is a better
   _____ for giving bad news?

10. What generation do you think _____ uses phones to talk
    most of the time?

REFLECT Brainstorm tips for texting.

You are going to read about tips for different types of communication,
including texting. Write five tips for older people about how to text younger
people. Share your tips with someone from an older generation. Are the
tips helpful? Then ask that person for tips about how to text older people.
Take notes. Then compare ideas in a group.

WHAT'S THE BEST CHOICE?

A mother celebrates her daughter's first birthday with friends and family with a virtual meeting in New York, NY, USA.

A PREDICT Read the first paragraph and the three headings. What do you think are the advantages and disadvantages of each type of communication? Then read and check your ideas.

1   Today, we share more information through technology. What is the best way to communicate clearly? The rules may depend on the type of communication—texting, email, or a virtual[1] meeting. Each type has its own advantages and disadvantages. To communicate well, we need to understand these differences.

Texting

2   Texting has many advantages. It's quick. You usually get an answer almost **immediately**. It's more informal and often more fun. It's better for close relationships. But it's not good for long messages or difficult ideas. Follow these **suggestions** for texting:

▸ **Reply** to **text messages** quickly.

▸ Be brief.

▸ Be careful texting when you're with other people. It may not be **polite**.

▸ Don't give bad news in a text.

Email

3   People **still** use email for longer messages, though it's not as popular with younger generations. There are several advantages. You can include more information. It gives people more time to answer. Email is more formal than texting. It is a good **choice** for more formal relationships, such as student and teacher. However, emails generally have a slower reply time. In emails, you should:

▸ Take **enough** time to answer carefully. If it is a group email, give others time to answer.

▸ Use the *To* line for the people you want to answer. Use the *CC* line for people who don't need to answer.

▸ Be clear in the *Subject* line. Write the topic of your email.

Virtual meetings

4   Virtual meetings—for work, school, etc.—have become more common. There are many benefits. You can see people's faces as they speak. You can hear their tone of voice. It is a good way to discuss difficult problems and make decisions. But organizing and preparing for the meeting takes time. Tips for virtual meetings include:

▸ Prepare before the meeting. Look over your notes.

▸ Put your camera at eye level or a little higher. Check your audio and video.

▸ Turn your microphone[2] and camera on or off, as needed. People usually mute[3] the microphone when they aren't talking.

▸ Let others share their ideas. Don't **interrupt** them.

5   Technology makes it possible for people to communicate across long **distances** quickly and easily. If you follow the rules for each type of contact, you will be much more successful.

---

[1] **virtual** (adj) using a computer or the Internet to make something appear real

[2] **microphone** (n) a piece of equipment that you speak into so others can hear you

[3] **mute** (v) to turn off the sound

B MAIN IDEAS Check (✓) the four main ideas.

1. _____ Different types of communication have different advantages.

2. _____ Texting can be fun.

3. _____ Texting is better for close relationships and short messages.

4. _____ Email is good for longer messages and formal relationships.

5. _____ Older people use email more than teenagers.

6. _____ You shouldn't interrupt speakers in virtual meetings.

7. _____ Because you can see people, virtual meetings are good for solving problems.

C DETAILS The article has five paragraphs. Write the paragraph number next to each detail. You can write a paragraph number more than once.

a. _____ Put the camera at eye level.

b. _____ Be clear in the *Subject* line.

c. _____ The *CC* line is for people who don't need to answer.

d. _____ Be brief.

e. _____ Look over notes to prepare.

f. _____ Answer quickly.

g. _____ Mute the microphone.

D APPLY Find the underlined pronouns in the reading. Complete the sentences.

1. The pronoun *It* in paragraph 2 refers to _____.

2. The pronoun *they* in paragraph 4 refers to _____.

CRITICAL THINKING   Determine appropriate communication

To communicate successfully, it is important to choose the **appropriate tone** and **type** of communication. Ask:

▶ Is the relationship with the other person formal or informal?
▶ Is the relationship with someone who is older or in a higher position?
▶ Does the person prefer to receive text messages or emails?

Formal language usually includes longer sentences, more formal words, and full forms, not contractions. When you write to someone in a higher position, use correct grammar, punctuation, and spelling.

REFLECT   Choose appropriate communication.

Write a text message or email to two different people: a close friend and an older relative, a teacher, or a boss. Explain that you will be late for an event with them the next day. Don't say who each message is for. Then exchange with a partner. Identify the people your partner wrote to and give feedback on his/her communication choices.

WRITE

Write a formal email.

You are going to write an email to a teacher. This is a common way to communicate in an academic setting. Use the ideas, vocabulary, and skills from the unit.

A MODEL Read the email. Underline the subject.

To: Adam.Sharma@anyu.edu
Cc:
Bcc:
Subject: EFL 103, Section 2—Project Topic

Dear Dr. Sharma,
This is Halima Jones from your EFL 103, Section 2 class. I'm working on the project for next week, and I have some questions.

I'm going to be at school tomorrow. Will you be available to meet sometime in the afternoon?

Thank you for your time. I look forward to hearing from you.

Best regards,
Halima Jones

WRITING SKILL Write an email to a teacher

Writing an email to a teacher is an important skill. Reasons to email a teacher include:

- asking a question about an assignment or test
- scheduling a meeting
- sending a written assignment

Use a formal tone. Don't use texting language. Instead, use complete sentences and correct spelling and punctuation. Remember to:
- clearly identify your topic in the *Subject* line
- give your full name and include your class
- make your message brief and clear
- use a polite greeting (*Dear Professor/Dr./Mr./Ms. Sharma*) and closing (*Best regards* or *Sincerely*)

To discuss complex or difficult ideas or problems, such as a grade or something personal, it's usually best to schedule a face-to-face meeting.

B ANALYZE THE MODEL Complete the outline of the model email.

1. **Subject:** _____

2. **Greeting:** _____

3. **Body:**

   a. Identify self: _____

   b. Give background information: _____

   _____

   c. State purpose/Ask a question: _____

   _____

4. **Concluding sentence(s):** _____

5. **Closing:** _____

GRAMMAR Review of the present continuous

We use the **present continuous** to talk about things that are happening now.

   The Internet **is changing** writing in many ways.

To form the present continuous, use *am/are/is* (+ *not*) + verb + *-ing*.

   You**'re not communicating** clearly. You**'re speaking** too fast.

   Taylor **is playing** with her brother right now. She **isn't studying**.

   Teenagers (14–18) **are leading** the change. They **aren't following** others.

We use the present continuous with time expressions such as *now*, *right now*, *at the moment*, and *this month/year*.

C GRAMMAR Complete the sentences with the present continuous of the verbs.

1. I _____ (email) my teacher about the final project.

2. The group members _____ (try) to find a good topic.

3. We _____ (not, listen) to each other.

4. I _____ (prepare) my notes for a virtual meeting now.

5. You _____ (not, mute) your microphone right now.

6. Eva _____ (plan) her weekend schedule at the moment.

GRAMMAR Review of the future

We use *be going to* and *will* to talk about the **future**.

We use *be going to* with plans and predictions. Use *am/are/is* (+ *not*) + *going to* + base form.

> I **am going to study** hard this semester. (plan)
>
> She**'s** probably **going to check** her phone tonight. (prediction)
>
> We**'re not going to interrupt** our classmates anymore. (plan)
>
> **Are** people **going to decrease** their use of technology? (prediction)

We use *will* for offers and predictions. Use *will* (+ *not*) + base form. You can use the contraction *'ll* with subject pronouns.

> I **will help** you with the homework assignment. (offer)
>
> Internet language **won't stay** the same. (prediction)
>
> We**'ll give** you suggestions for your new website. (offer)
>
> **Will** you **receive** a good grade next week? (prediction)

Use the future with expressions such as *tomorrow, next week, in 10 years,* and *in the future.*

D GRAMMAR Complete the sentences with a future form of the verbs. Use *be going to* in sentences 1–5. Use *will* in sentences 6–10.

1. In the future, people _____ (miss) face-to-face meetings.

2. I _____ (reply) to the message tomorrow.

3. We _____ (not, use) the same punctuation 10 years from now.

4. The teacher _____ (not, assign) homework this weekend.

5. They _____ (study) harder for the next test.

6. He _____ (join) the virtual meeting soon.

7. It _____ (not, start) immediately.

8. You _____ (need) a microphone.

9. Language _____ (change) from one generation to the next.

10. Technology _____ (provide) new choices for communication.

E GRAMMAR Choose the correct words to complete the email.

Dear Dr. Lee,

I'm in your ENG 101 class. I'm ¹**read / reading** my notes from class today. I don't understand a few things.

According to the schedule, you're going ²**give / to give** us a test next Thursday on this topic. I ³**won't / not going to** have enough time on Tuesday after class to talk then. Some classmates and I ⁴**am / are** going to study this weekend.

Are you going to ⁵**be / being** in your office tomorrow? If so, could I stop by to discuss?

Thank you for your time.

Best regards,
Jason Oluo

F GRAMMAR Answer the questions with your ideas.

1. What classes are you going to take next?

   _____

2. How do you think classes will change in the next few years? Explain.

   _____

3. What will you do when you finish school?

   _____

G EDIT Read the email. Find and correct one error with the present progressive, three errors with the future, and two examples of informal language.

Hey Professor Tsao,

I'm in Eng 203. I'm study for the final test, and I have some questions. Will we having to write a paragraph on the final?

Also, I going to Peru next week. I will not to be here on Friday for the final. Is it possible to take the test early?

CU L8R,
Tomas Milan

PLAN & WRITE

H BRAINSTORM Review the Writing Skill, including reasons to email the teacher. What do you want to email a teacher about? Write at least three ideas below. Then choose one as the topic for your email.

_____

_____

_____

I OUTLINE Complete the outline.

1. **Subject:** _____

2. **Greeting:** _____

3. **Body:**

   a. Identify self: _____

   b. Give background information: _____

   _____

   c. State purpose/Ask a question: _____

   _____

4. **Concluding sentence(s):** _____

5. **Closing:** _____

J FIRST DRAFT Use your outline to write a first draft of your email.

K REVISE Use this list to write your second draft.

- ☐ Does your subject line give clear information?
- ☐ Do you use a formal tone throughout?
- ☐ Do you identify yourself?
- ☐ Are your greeting and closing polite?
- ☐ Are there any details you need to add?
- ☐ Is there any information that is not relevant to the topic?

L EDIT Use this list as you write your final draft.

- ☐ Do you use the present continuous and the future correctly?
- ☐ Do your subjects and verbs agree?
- ☐ Do you spell all the words correctly?
- ☐ Do you use correct capitalization and punctuation?

M FINAL DRAFT Reread your final draft and correct any errors. Then submit it to your teacher.

REFLECT

A Check (✓) the Reflect activities you can do and the academic skills you can use.

☐ analyze communication across generations

☐ communicate tone in a message

☐ brainstorm tips for texting

☐ choose appropriate communication

☐ write a formal email

☐ understand pronoun reference

☐ write an email to a teacher

☐ review of the present continuous

☐ review of the future

☐ determine appropriate communication

B Check (✓) the vocabulary words from the unit that you know. Circle words you still need to practice. Add any other words that you learned.

NOUN	VERB	ADJECTIVE	ADVERB & OTHER
choice	interrupt	enough	generally
comment	reply	informal	immediately
distance	shout	polite	probably
generation		required	still
purpose			
sort			
suggestion			
technology			
text message			

C Reflect on the ideas in the unit as you answer these questions.

1. In what ways could you communicate better through text messages, email, or virtual meetings?

   _____

   _____

2. What ideas or skills in this unit will be most useful to you in the future?

   _____

   _____

Using a dictionary Example sentences

In addition to a definition, dictionaries will usually show a word in an example sentence. You can use the example sentence to better understand how the word is used. An example sentence also gives clues to the words that collocate (or go) with the target word.

area /ˈɛriə/ *n.* **1** [C] a place, location: *The picnic area is near the parking lot.* ‖ *The New York area has high rents.* **2** [C] part of a room or a building: *My kitchen has a dining area.* ‖ *My apartment building has a storage area in the basement.*

A Use a dictionary. Write an example sentence for each word.

1. basic (adj) _____

2. company (n) _____

3. goal (n) _____

4. sick (adj) _____

5. sell (v) _____

Polysemy Multiple-meaning words

"Polysemy" refers to a word that has two or more different meanings.

Sometimes the meanings are similar but not exactly the same. The noun *company*, for example, can mean "a business" or "companionship." Use context clues—the words before and after a word—to help you decide which is the correct meaning.

B Choose the best meaning for the words in bold. Check your answers in a dictionary.

1. I **believe** that this is the best community project ever.

    a. think   b. have religious faith

2. The new design looks **terrible!** The colors are too bright and ugly.

    a. bad   b. difficult

3. The firefighter is a **hero**. The news report said she saved someone's life.

    a. main character in a story   b. brave person

4. There isn't any green **space** in my neighborhood.

    a. area beyond Earth   b. area used for something

5. For a politician, losing an election has got to **hurt**.

    a. feel physical pain   b. be emotionally difficult

Suffix -ity

A suffix is a group of letters that comes at the end of a word. A suffix changes the part of speech, or form, of a word.

The suffix -ity means "state" or "condition." You can add it to some adjectives to change them to nouns. For adjectives ending in -ble, replace -le with -ility.

ADJECTIVE   NOUN

Two things are <u>similar</u>. = Two things have <u>a similar**ity**</u>.

Something is <u>possible</u>. = There is <u>a possib**ility**</u>.

A   Add -ity to each adjective to make nouns. Use a dictionary to check your spelling.

Adjectives	Nouns
1. active	_____
2. electric	_____
3. popular	_____
4. positive	_____
5. possible	_____

Polysemy Multiple-meaning words

Remember: The term "polysemy" refers to a word that has two or more different meanings.

The noun *head*, for example, can mean "a person in charge" or "the body part above your neck." Sometimes one word can also be different parts of speech. The word *head* can also be a verb meaning *to lead*. Use context clues—the words before and after a word—to help you decide which is the correct meaning.

B   Choose the best meaning of the words in bold. Check your answers in a dictionary.

1. I wear **casual** clothes when I'm relaxing with friends.

    a. informal   b. not serious

2. We are friends because of our **common** interest in skateboarding.

    a. ordinary   b. shared by two or more people

3. Even during hard times, my friend always has a **positive** attitude.

    a. meaning yes   b. full of hope

4. I think it's **strange** that my friend doesn't like pizza. Most people think it's delicious.

    a. not usual   b. not known

5. This shirt doesn't **fit**. It's too small.

    a. be in good physical shape   b. be the right size

Onomatopoeia Words that make noises

Some words in English sound like the noise of the thing that they are describing. For example, the pronunciation of *hiss* sounds like the noise a snake makes. These kinds of words are examples of onomatopoeia.

A   Match the word with the sound it describes. Check your answers in a dictionary.

1. click _____
2. bang _____
3. beep _____
4. buzz _____
5. ding _____

     a. a metallic sound like a bell
     b. a sound like a car horn or electronic device
     c. a sudden loud noise
     d. a light snapping sound
     e. a sound like a bee

Using a dictionary Synonyms

Synonyms are words that are similar in meaning. The words *small* and *little* are synonyms. A dictionary may include synonyms in a box labeled *Thesaurus* or marked with the abbreviation *SYN*. You can also look for synonyms in a thesaurus.

THESAURUS

memory *n.* recollection, remembrance

B   Use a dictionary. Match the words that are synonyms.

1. modern _____
2. noisy _____
3. popular _____
4. quiet _____
5. useful _____

     a. practical
     b. contemporary
     c. silent
     d. loud
     e. well-liked

Prefixes *col-* and *com-*

A prefix is a group of letters that comes at the beginning of a word. It changes the meaning of the word. The prefixes *com-* and *col-* usually mean "with" or "together." For example, *communicate* means "to talk with someone."

When you see a new word beginning with *col-* or *com-*, you have a clue to help you understand the meaning.

A Match the words in bold with the correct definitions. Use a dictionary if necessary.

1. Academic journals **collect** research papers from different scientists in their publications.
2. To make pancakes, first **combine** eggs, flour, milk, and butter.
3. I like many of my **colleagues** at work. We often eat lunch together.
4. Please **complete** this exercise for homework.
5. When researcher **compare** the two groups, the results are different.

   a. _____ (v) to look for the differences between two things

   b. _____ (v) to mix together

   c. _____ (v) to bring together in an organized way

   d. _____ (v) to finish with

   e. _____ (n) people you work with

Base words and affixes

A base word is a word that can't be broken into smaller words. For example, the verb *equip* is a base word. You can add affixes—suffixes or prefixes—to a base word to change its meaning or form.

equip + ***ment*** = *equipment*   ***re*** + ***equip*** = *reequip*

A dictionary will often list common affixes that you can add to a base word.

B Add the correct prefix or suffix from the box to each word. Use a dictionary to help you. Make sure any change is spelled correctly. Then write a brief explanation of each new word.

-al	-ate	dis-	-ify	-ly	un-

1. fortune _fortunate Fortunate means lucky._____

2. brief _____

3. profession _____

4. advantage _____

5. available _____

6. simple _____

Word roots *bene*, *sect*, and *tract*

Many words in English come from Latin word roots. Knowing the meaning of Latin word roots can help you understand the meaning of unfamiliar vocabulary.

Latin *tract*, meaning "pull" as in **attract**
Latin *bene*, meaning "good" or "well" as in **benefit**
Latin *sect*, meaning "cut" as in **section**

A Choose the best answer for the words in bold. Use the root word to help. Then check your answers in a dictionary.

1. Farmers often drive **tractors** around their farms.

   A **tractor** is probably used to _____.

   a. feed small animals   b. move heavy farm machinery   c. travel long distances

2. An important **sector** of the economy is manufacturing.

   A **sector** probably means _____.

   a. a part of a larger thing   b. every part   c. a small part

3. Eating fruits and vegetables is **beneficial** to your health.

   If something is beneficial it is probably a(n) _____ thing.

   a. negative   b. unimportant   c. positive

Collocations Adjective + *food*

Collocations are two or more words that often go together. It is useful to learn collocations in the way you learn an individual word. Here are some common collocations with the noun *food*.

convenience food: pre-prepared snacks and meals that are ready-to-eat
fast food: food that can be made and eaten quickly at a restaurant
fresh food: food picked or produced recently and not preserved
junk food: food that tastes good but is bad for your health
natural food: food made without artificial ingredients added
organic food: food using crops grown without chemicals

B Complete the chart with the collocations from the box above.

Types of food that are good for us	Types of food that are not good for us

Prefix *re-*

Remember: A prefix is a group of letters that comes at the beginning of a word that changes the meaning of the word. The prefix *re-* means "again." You can add *re-* to some verbs to show that the action is being done again.

re + *view* = ***re****view*, meaning "to look at (view) something again"

A Match the verbs with the correct definition. Check your answers in a dictionary.

1. replace _____   a. to move to a new place

2. reuse _____   b. to use something again in a different way

3. rebuild _____   c. to consider something again

4. relocate _____   d. to have something take the place of something else

5. rethink _____   e. to make something again

Suffixes *-ing* and *-ive*

Remember: A suffix is a group of letters that comes at the end of a word. You can change some verbs to adjectives by adding suffixes such as *-ing* and *-ive*.

The suffix *-ive* means "having the quality." The suffix *-ing* means "having the effect on something."

interest + *-ing* = *interest****ing***   NOT ~~interestive~~
secret + *-ive* = *secret****ive***   NOT ~~secreting~~

Words that end in *-ing* and *-ed* can be adjectives or verb forms. Use the context to decide if the word is an adjective or verb

B Add the correct suffix to each verb to make adjectives. Use a dictionary to help you. Make sure any change is spelled correctly. Then write a brief explanation of each new word.

1. attract _____

2. create _____

3. damage _____

4. decrease _____

5. invent _____

6. protect_____

7. relax _____

8. surprise _____

Formal and informal language

In a professional or academic setting—such as in an essay—you are likely to use formal language. In casual or more personal settings, you may use less formal language. The words you choose can show this difference.

More formal: Her main **occupation** is as an inventor.

More informal: She has a cool **job**. She's an inventor!

More formal: He **regretted** his mistake.

More informal: He **was sorry about** his mistake.

In formal writing, you often use longer, single words than in informal writing. You also don't use spoken expressions or phrases, for example, "sorry about."

A Match the formal word with the correct informal word or phrase. Check your answers in a dictionary.

MORE FORMAL

1. finally _____
2. pleasant _____
3. not attend _____
4. demonstrate _____
5. relocate _____
6. collect _____

MORE INFORMAL

a. show
b. miss
c. nice
d. in the end
e. pick up
f. move

Prefix *pre-*

Remember: A prefix is a group of letters that comes at the beginning of a word that changes the meaning of the word. The prefix *pre-* means "before." You can add *pre-* to some words to create new words.

pre + *view* = **pre**view, meaning "to view or watch beforehand."

Some words already begin with *pre-*.

predict   **pre**pare   **pre**vent

When you see a new word beginning with *pre-*, you have a clue to help you understand the meaning.

B Guess the meaning of the words in the box. Then check the definitions in a dictionary.

predict	prepare	prepay	preschool	preteen	prevent

C Complete each sentence with one of the words from the box in **B**. One word is extra.

1. Before children start elementary school, they often go to _____.

2. It is a good idea to _____ your notes and PowerPoint slides before a presentation.

3. Before reading an article, it's a good idea to _____ what it will be about. Looking at the title and photos can help.

4. To _____ arguments at work, be polite with your co-workers.

5. You usually have to _____ when you order food online. Have your credit card ready!

Using a dictionary Idioms

An idiom is a multi-word expression that is hard to define just by looking at each word. Most idioms are informal language.

A dictionary may include the common idioms under the expression's main word. For example, the video in Unit 8 uses the idiom *have (got) something covered.*

have (got) someone or something **covered**

to provide whatever is needed; to take care of everything

Don't worry about picking up the kids tonight. I've got you covered.

A Use a dictionary. Match the definitions to the correct idioms.

1. to write a message _____
2. to start doing something that others copy _____
3. to spend time with someone _____
4. on the whole; generally _____
5. immediately; very quickly _____

a. in a flash
b. hang out with
c. by and large
d. drop a line
e. set a trend

Collocations *Send* and *make* + noun

Collocations are two or more words that often go together. It's useful to learn collocations in the same way you learn an individual word.

The verbs *send* and *make* often collocate with particular nouns. For example, you can *send a message*, but you can't *make a message*. Some nouns collocate with both *send* and *make*.

send	make	send / make
a reply	a call	a suggestion
a message	a choice	a comment

B Underline the collocations in the examples. Then answer the questions.

1. Who sent a text message to you yesterday? _____

2. Did you send a reply? What did it say? _____

3. When did you last make a call to a friend? _____

4. Do you like it when your teacher makes comments about your essay? Why? _____

5. When did you last make a suggestion? What was it? _____

VOCABULARY INDEX

Unit 1	Page	CEFR	Unit 3	Page	CEFR
area*	5	A2	actually	41	A2
basic	9	B1	background	41	B1
believe	9	A2	certain	41	B1
company	9	A2	click*	45	A2
dangerous	5	A2	communicate*	45	B1
dirty	5	A2	concentrate*	41	B1
earn	9	A2	culture*	45	B1
emergency	5	B1	experience	45	B1
goal*	9	B1	however	45	A2
hero	9	B1	memory	41	B1
hurt	5	A2	modern	45	A2
medicine	5	A2	noisy*	41	A2
organization	9	B1	popular	45	A2
price	9	A2	quiet	41	A2
project*	9	A2	repeat	41	A2
sell	9	A2	solve	41	B1
sick	5	A2	sound	41	A2
space	5	A2	type	45	A2
storm	5	A2	useful	45	A2
terrible	5	A2	volume*	45	B1

Unit 2	Page	CEFR	Unit 4	Page	CEFR
activity	23	A2	advice	63	A2
afterward	27	A2	available*	59	A2
become	23	A2	brief*	63	B1
casual	23	B1	check	63	A2
common	27	B1	colleague*	63	A2
connect	23	B1	collect	59	B1
contact*	27	A2	diary*	59	A2
decide	27	A2	disadvantage*	59	B1
find out	27	A2	discover	63	B1
fit	27	A2	equipment*	63	B1
happen	27	A2	exactly	63	A2
improve	23	A2	free	59	A2
introduce	23	B1	join	63	A2
opinion	27	B1	nature	59	A2
positive	23	B1	nearly	63	A2
research*	23	B1	pattern	63	B1
strange	27	A2	professional*	59	B1
stranger	23	B1	report	59	B1
successful	27	B1	task	59	B1
variety	23	A2	unfortunately	59	A2

*Academic words

VOCABULARY INDEX

Unit 5	Page	CEFR
attract	77	B1
carefully	81	A2
convince*	77	B1
customer	77	A2
diet	81	B1
encourage	81	B1
fast food	81	A2
give up	77	B1
include	81	A2
instead	77	A2
label*	77	B1
menu	77	A2
natural	81	B1
negative	81	A2
option*	81	B1
order	77	A2
product	81	B1
section*	77	B1
select	81	B1
whole	81	A2

Unit 7	Page	CEFR
amount	113	B1
depend on	113	B1
employer	117	B1
even	113	A2
feeling	113	B1
finally*	113	A2
interview	117	B1
judge	117	B1
miss	117	A2
motivated	113	B2
offer	117	A2
organize	117	B1
pay attention	113	B1
pick up	117	A2
pleasant	113	A2
prepare	113	A2
realize	117	B1
receive	117	A2
recent	113	B1
serious	117	B1

Unit 6	Page	CEFR
at least	99	A2
the country	95	A2
crime	95	B1
damage	99	B1
decrease	95	B1
history	99	A2
list	99	A2
outdoors	95	B1
perhaps	95	A2
prevent	95	B1
protect	99	B1
region*	99	B1
replace	99	B1
site*	99	B1
spend time	95	A2
stress*	95	B1
tourist	99	A2
view	95	A2
wonderful	99	A2
woods	95	A2

Unit 8	Page	CEFR
choice	135	B1
comment	131	B1
distance	135	B1
enough	135	A2
generally	131	B1
generation*	131	B1
immediately	135	A2
informal	131	B2
interrupt	135	B1
polite	135	A2
probably	131	A2
purpose	131	B1
reply	135	B1
required	131	B1
shout	131	A2
sort	131	A2
still	135	A2
suggestion	135	B1
technology*	131	B1
text message*	135	A2

SENTENCE TYPES

There are three types of sentences: simple, compound, and complex. These labels refer to how a sentence is organized, not how difficult the content is.

SIMPLE SENTENCES

Simple sentences contain a subject (s) and a verb (v). They have just one independent clause. An independent clause can stand alone.

       S   V

Bats are interesting animals.

      V   S   V

Do you like bats?

Simple sentences can contain more than one subject or verb.

      S   S   V

Bats and dolphins are mammals.

      S   V   V

Bats are nocturnal and have good night vision.

COMPOUND SENTENCES

Compound sentences contain at least two independent clauses (ic). These two clauses are combined with a connector called a *coordinating conjunction* (cc), such as *and, but, or, yet, so,* and *for.* Use a comma before the connector connecting two independent clauses.

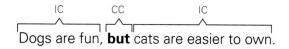

       IC   CC   IC

Dogs are fun, **but** cats are easier to own.

          IC   CC   IC

Lea worked hard on the project, **so** she got a good grade.

COMPLEX SENTENCES

Complex sentences contain one independent clause (IC) and at least one dependent clause (DC). A dependent clause cannot stand alone. In some complex sentences, the dependent clause is an adverb clause. Adverb clauses begin with connectors called *subordinating conjunctions,* such as *while, although, because,* and *if.* Note that if a sentence begins with an independent clause, there is not a comma separating the two clauses. If a sentence begins with a dependent clause, there is a comma.

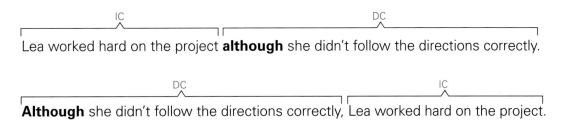

EDITING TIPS

Capitalize:

- ▶ the first word of every sentence.
- ▶ the pronoun *I.*
- ▶ people's titles, e.g., Ms., Mr., Mrs., Dr.
- ▶ proper names of people, places, and organizations.
- ▶ locations, e.g., street names, cities, states, countries, and rivers.
- ▶ days, months, and holidays.
- ▶ the names of languages and nationalities.

Punctuate:

- ▶ with a period (.) at the end of every sentence that is not a question.
- ▶ with a question mark (?) at the end of every sentence that is a question.
- ▶ with an exclamation mark (!) to show strong feelings. This is not used often in academic writing.
- ▶ with commas (,) to separate a list of three or more things and after some introductory words or phrases, e.g., *Hopefully, However, Finally,* and *Meanwhile,.*
- ▶ with a comma before combining words joining two sentences, e.g., *and, but, so,* and *or.*
- ▶ with an apostrophe (') to show possession.
- ▶ with quotation marks (" ") to show that you are using someone's exact words.

IRREGULAR VERB FORMS

Base form	Simple past	Past participle
be	was, were	been
beat	beat	beaten
become	became	become
begin	began	begun
bend	bent	bent
bite	bit	bitten
blow	blew	blown
break	broke	broken
bring	brought	brought
build	built	built
buy	bought	bought
catch	caught	caught
choose	chose	chosen
come	came	come
cost	cost	cost
cut	cut	cut
dig	dug	dug
dive	dived/dove	dived
do	did	done
draw	drew	drawn
drink	drank	drunk
drive	drove	driven
eat	ate	eaten
fall	fell	fallen
feed	fed	fed
feel	felt	felt
fight	fought	fought
find	found	found
fit	fit	fit/fitted
fly	flew	flown
forget	forgot	forgotten
forgive	forgave	forgiven
freeze	froze	frozen
get	got	got/gotten
give	gave	given
go	went	gone
grow	grew	grown
hang	hung	hung
have	had	had
hear	heard	heard
hide	hid	hidden
hit	hit	hit
hold	held	held
hurt	hurt	hurt
keep	kept	kept
know	knew	known

Base form	Simple past	Past participle
lay	laid	laid
lead	led	led
leave	left	left
lend	lent	lent
let	let	let
lie	lay	lain
light	lit/lighted	lit/lighted
lose	lost	lost
make	made	made
mean	meant	meant
meet	met	met
pay	paid	paid
prove	proved	proved/proven
put	put	put
quit	quit	quit
read	read	read
ride	rode	ridden
ring	rang	rung
rise	rose	risen
run	ran	run
say	said	said
sit	sat	sat
sleep	slept	slept
slide	slid	slid
speak	spoke	spoken
spend	spent	spent
spread	spread	spread
stand	stood	stood
steal	stole	stolen
stick	stuck	stuck
strike	struck	struck
swear	swore	sworn
sweep	swept	swept
swim	swam	swum
take	took	taken
teach	taught	taught
tear	tore	torn
tell	told	told
think	thought	thought
throw	threw	thrown
understand	understood	understood
upset	upset	upset
wake	woke	woken
wear	wore	worn
win	won	won
write	wrote	written

Reflect is designed to provide practice for standardized exams, such as IELTS and TOEFL. This book has many activities that focus on and practice skills and question types that are needed for test success.

READING • Key Skills	IELTS	TOEFL	Page(s)
Guess meaning from context	x	x	62, 66
Identify facts and opinions	x	x	80, 84
Identify supporting information	x	x	44, 84
Predict what you will read	x	x	42, 46, 60, 78, 96, 100, 132, 136
Preview a text	x	x	6, 10, 24, 28, 46, 64, 82, 114, 118
Read or scan for specific details	x	x	8, 12, 26, 29, 44, 48, 62, 66, 80, 84, 98, 102, 116, 119, 134, 138
Read or skim for main ideas	x	x	8, 12, 26, 29, 43, 47, 48, 60, 64, 79, 83, 96, 100, 115, 118, 133, 137
Understand paragraph structure	x	x	24
Understand pronoun reference		x	134, 138
Understand reasons	x	x	8
Understand the author's purpose		x	98

READING • Common Question Types	IELTS	TOEFL	Page(s)
Complete sentences or a table	x		12, 14, 30, 31, 50, 67, 80, 84, 85, 98, 116
Judge if details are true, false, or not given	x		8, 26, 60, 79, 102, 120, 133
Match information to a paragraph	x		26, 29, 43, 44, 48, 60, 83, 96, 115, 138
Match information to a category or person	x	x	8, 29, 43, 48, 80
Multiple choice or multiple response	x	x	12, 64, 98, 100, 137
Put information in order		x	68, 118, 123
Short answer	x		66

WRITING • Key Skills	IELTS	TOEFL	Page(s)
Analyze graphs and charts	x		101, 102, 105, 117
Brainstorm ideas	x	x	17, 35, 53, 89, 125, 135, 143
Describe data	x		103, 108, 117
Organize a paragraph	x	x	31
Plan or outline what you will write	x	x	18, 35, 53, 71, 90, 107, 143
Review and edit to fix errors	x	x	17, 34, 52, 70, 88, 106, 125, 142
Support opinions with reasons	x	x	26, 89
Write about the steps in a process	x	x	68, 71
Write a paragraph	x	x	18, 36, 54, 68, 72, 90, 108, 123, 126
Write coherently	x	x	122
Write concluding sentences	x	x	35, 53, 71, 86, 90, 107, 126, 143
Write supporting sentences	x	x	35, 49, 53, 71, 90, 126
Write topic sentences	x	x	32, 35, 53, 71, 90, 126

WRITING • Common Topics	IELTS	TOEFL	Page(s)
Advertising and business	x	x	90
Communities	x	x	18
Friends and family	x	x	36
Music and entertainment	x		54
Success and failure	x	x	126

CREDITS

Illustration: All illustrations are owned by © Cengage.

Cover © Lorenz Holder; **2–3** (spread) © Randy Fath/Unsplash.com; **4** © RogerAllen/SplashNews; **6–7** (spread) © PhilYeomans/BNPS; **10–11** (spread) © Kyle Miller Creative; **13** Ian Dagnall/Alamy Stock Photo; **15** robertharding/Alamy Stock Photo; **16** Placebo365/E+/Getty Images; **20–21** (spread) DLILLC/Corbis/VCG/Getty Images; **22** aberCPC/Alamy Stock Photo; **24–25** (spread) © Susan Seubert; **28–29** (spread) iStock.com/yogysic; **30** © Susan Seubert; **34** Klaus Vedfelt/DigitalVision/Getty Images; **36** Maskot/Getty Images; **38–39** (spread) Nikada/iStock Unreleased/Getty Images; **40** © Great Big Story; **42–43** (spread) Chip East/Reuters; **46–47** (spread) Isaac Lawrence/AFP/Getty Images; **49** Blend Images/Jeremy Woodhouse/Brand X Pictures/Getty Images; **52** Westend61/Getty Images; **54** Pekic/E+/Getty Images; **56–57** (spread) © Cristina Mittermeier; **58** © David Bodenham; **60–61** (spread) Joel Sartore/National Geographic Image Collection; **64** (bl) Courtesy of Venture Photography; **64–65** (spread) NASA; **67** Tashi-Delek/E+/Getty Images; **70** serkan mutan/Shutterstock.com; **71** (cl1) South China Morning Post/Getty Images, (cr1) Dylan Becksholt/Alamy Stock Photo, (cl2) Lee Chee Keong/EyeEm/Getty Images, (cr2) Olena Khudiakova/Ukrinform/Barcroft Media/Getty Images; **72** Christophe Merceron/Shutterstock.com; **74–75** (spread) © Marta Fowlie aka Food Polka; **76** National Geographic Image Collection; **78** (cr) vvmich/Fotosearch LBRF/AGE Fotostock; **78–79** (spread) Courtesy of freepik.com; **82** Paulo Fridman/Bloomberg/Getty Images; **88** Courtesy of The Advertising Archives; **92–93** (spread) Barcroft Media/Getty Images; **94** Efired/Shutterstock.com; **96–97** (spread) Steve McCurry/Magnum Photos New York; **100** © Iurie Belegurschi; **104** Gw. Nam/Moment/Getty Images; **108** Nick Fitzhardinge/Moment/Getty Images; **110–111** (spread) John Stillwell/PA Images/Getty Images; **112** Gabby Salazar/National Geographic Image Collection; **114–115** (spread) © Reed Young; **118–119** (spread) Zhang Qiao/VCG/Getty Images; **121** PhotoAlto/Alamy Stock Photo; **124** Rich Kane Photography/Alamy Stock Photo; **128–129** (spread) Gunnar Knechtel/laif/Redux; **130** Zhang Peng/LightRocket/Getty Images; **132** Dina Litovsky/National Geographic Image Collection; **136** Thomas Dworzak/Magnum Photos New York; **144** Adam Bronkhorst/Alamy Stock Photo.